IRELAND OF THE PROVERB

Ireland of the Proverb

Liam Mac Con Iomaire

Photographs by Bill Doyle

MASTERS PRESS

Published by Masters Press, 5460 33rd Street, S.E., Grand Rapids, Michigan 49508

Printed in the United States of America

Library of Congress Cataloging-in-Publication Data

Mac Con Iomaire, Liam.
Ireland of the proverb / Liam Mac Con Iomaire.
  p.   cm.
Text in English and Irish.
Bibliography: p.
ISBN 0-940279-23-1

  1. Proverbs, Irish. 2. Folklore–Ireland. 3. Ireland–Social
life and customs. I. Title.
PN6505.C5M33 1988
398′.9′2109415–dc19   88-13232 CIP

All photographs are by Bill Doyle except for the following:

Bord Fáilte: p. ix, 5, 22, 30 (upper right), 34, 39, 50 (upper right), 51, 53, 54, 55, 61 (lower), 67, 70 (upper right), 101, 102, 114, 116, 119, 123, 150, 166, 172 (upper right)
Jim Davis, The Boston Herald: p. 11
Tomás O'Muircheartaigh: p. 17
Caoimhín Ó Danachair: p. 4 (for the Irish Folklore Commission), p. 23, 225
RTÉ Illustrations Library: p. 61 (upper), 134, 135
National Museum of Ireland, Dublin: p. 70 (lower left)
A.C.O.T.: p. 78
Ake Campbell, Roinn Bhéaloideas Éireann, p. 146
Seamus O Duilearga: p. 147
Irish Times: p. 169, 171
Proinsias Ó Conluain: p. 185
Maurice Curtin, for The Irish Folklore Commission: p. 207

Cover and text design by Richard Hollick

Frontispiece: Near Dingle, Co. Kerry

Contents

Acknowledgments

I wish to thank the following for supplying additional photographs: Roinn Bhéaloideas Éireann (Department of Irish Folklore), University College, Dublin; Bord Fáilte Éireann (Irish Tourism Board); Radio Telefís Éireann; The Irish Times; An Bord Iascaigh Mhara (Irish Sea Fisheries Board); Irish Coursing Club; Ard-Mhúsaem na hÉireann (National Museum of Ireland); A.C.O.T. (Council for Development in Agriculture); Éamon de Buitléar, David Shaw-Smith and Proinsias Ó Conluain, and Comhairle Bhéaloideas Éireann for permission to use extracts from *Seán Ó Conaill's Book*.

I also wish to thank the following for their generous assistance: Anna Bale and Siobhán Ní Laoire of the Department of Modern Irish, University College, Dublin; Professor Bo Almqvist, Ríonach Uí Ógáin and Bairbre Ó Floinn of the Department of Irish Folklore, University College, Dublin; Brelda Baum, Mary Murphy and Mícheál Ó Muircheartaigh of R.T.É.; Paddy Putty of Bord Fáilte Éireann; Máire Davitt; Bríd Ní Threasaigh; and most of all Micil Pheadair Uí Nia agus a chlann from Doire Né Chasla, Co. na Gaillimhe.

A cassette tape of the author reading, in his native language, all the Irish phrases and proverbs in this book is available from the publisher for $8.95 plus $1.50 shipping and handling.

Introduction

Irish is my first language. Proverbs in Irish were an integral part of ordinary speech in my childhood days in the Connemara Gaeltacht in West Galway. I remember at a very young age, together with an older brother and sister, being allowed to help my mother place a clutch of eggs under a brooding hen. We had each put our own mark on four eggs, together with the sign of the cross for good luck. During the three long weeks we were waiting for the eggs to hatch, we were frequently told, "Don't count your chickens until they are hatched" (*Ná comhair do chuid sicíní go dtaga siad amach*). The three weeks eventually came to an end and twelve beautiful fluffy chicks were hatched out of the shells. The miracle was complete and we were prouder than the brooding hen.

My reason for mentioning this childhood memory is that I thought then that the advice about not counting our chickens was just a piece of parental wisdom. It was only later when I heard neighbors use the same expression in a different context, and heard outsiders use an English version of it, that I realized that it was a wise old saying or a proverb. I knew then that this and other catchy sayings I had heard my parents use so often were not exclusively theirs but belonged to everybody in the community.

Conversations between ordinary people were enriched by these sayings. The person who quoted a suitable proverb to sum up a situation or to suggest a certain course of action commanded respect in the community. Such a person was considered to be rich in conventional wisdom, and his or her use of proverbs was as worthy of respect as the use of textbooks by the formally educated. The proverbs were like a set of rules the community shared for reasoning with one another.

Many people have tried to use proverbs to define national or racial temperament, and many people believe the words of Francis Bacon that "the genius, wit and spirit of a nation are discovered in its proverbs." There are others, however, who believe this is a futile exercise, because vast numbers of proverbs in any one language are also found in many other languages. Proverbs, like much folklore, are to a large extent international. Many of them have been passed from mouth to mouth, from generation to generation, from country to country, over hundreds and thousands of years. The same proverb can be found, with possible variations, all over the world. It is fascinating to think how long any one proverb has been in existence and how far around the world it has travelled. Many proverbs have their origin in the Bible, many come from the Latin writers, and many come from an earlier vernacular source or tradition.

Some of the best proverbs are ones that seem to be observations on animals or birds, but are in reality observations on human behavior. Irish proverbs frequently refer to farmyard animals and fowl. The hen and the cow, not surprisingly, are often mentioned, as so many generations of the rural poor depended on them for food and sustenance. When we hear "The hen has ruffled feathers until she rears her brood" (*Is gliobach í an chearc go dtógann sí a hál*), we recognize it as an observation on the poor mother who is struggling to rear a big family. The selfish person is compared to the cat, the dim-witted to the donkey, and the diligent, hard-working person to the much-respected horse. Inanimate objects are also used in comparisons: "When fire is put to the rock, it cracks" (*Nuair a chuirtear tine leis an gcloch pléascann sí*) suggests that we all have our breaking point, and "The barrel that contains the wine will retain a drop in its staves" (*An bairille a mbíonn an fíon ann, fanann an braon sna cláir*) sounds more lyrical to me than "a chip off the old block."

Rhyme and rhythm are very prevalent in Irish proverbs, and many of them may have been composed or adapted by folk poets. Brevity is also a common trait and very often the proverb is pruned down to a minimum of three, or even two, words: "Necessity is the mother of invention" (*Múineann gá seift*), or "A bad egg, a bad bird" (*Drochubh, drochéan*).

It is true that proverbs are not as widely used in the Gaeltacht areas today as they were in the past, nevertheless, every fluent native Irish speaker possesses a considerable repertoire of proverbs. Professor Bo Almqvist, head of the Department of Irish Folklore in University College Dublin, collected 1,500 proverbs from one man, Mícheál Ó Guithín, from the Great Blasket Island, Kerry, over a period of eight years and his repertoire had by no means been exhausted when he died in 1974. The man's mother, Peig Sayers, had an even greater store of proverbs, and her books *Peig* (an autobiography) and *Machtnamh Seana-Mhná (An Old Woman's Reflections)* contain a great number of them. Both books are available in English translation.

Most, if not all, of the proverbs in this collection are still being used by native Irish speakers in the Gaeltacht (Irish-speaking) districts of Donegal, Mayo, Galway, Kerry, Cork, Waterford, and Meath and have counterparts in Scots Gaelic. Nearly all of them are to be found in *Seanfhocail Chonnacht (The Proverbs of Connacht)*, edited by T. S. Ó Máille; *Seanfhocail Uladh (The Proverbs of Ulster)*, edited by E. Ó Muirgheasa; *Seanfhocail na Mumhan (The Proverbs of Munster)*, edited by An Seabhac; and *A Miscellany of Irish Proverbs*, edited by T. F. O'Rahilly.

This collection forms a good cross section of Irish proverbs, and I have grouped them under ten different subject headings. At the outset, in a section I call "Introductory Proverbs," I have selected ten proverbs which, with the aid of the accompanying photographs and text, will help to introduce the stranger to life in Ireland as it used to be. Toward the back of the book I have included a short collection of numerical proverbs called triads and a short collection of quotation proverbs. Underneath the original Irish text of each proverb I give an English translation. The availability of "matching" photographs did, of course, have a bearing on my selection, but I hope that this has not prevented me from bringing you some of the best of Irish proverbs.

The Irish Language

Irish (*Gaeilge*) was the language of the Irish people for two thousand years. Since the seventeenth century, however, it has been receding before English and is today a minority language, spoken as a community language only in the isolated and shrinking rural districts we call the Gaeltacht. Although Irish is the first language of more than 100,000 people in the country as a whole, it is estimated that no more than 25,000 of the Gaeltacht population now speak Irish consistently as their day-to-day language. It is taught in nearly all the schools and is the chosen literary medium of a small but talented group of writers. Although 31.6 percent of the total population was returned as Irish-speaking in the 1981 census, this is more an indicator of a capacity to speak Irish than it is of its actual use.

Historically speaking, Irish is an Indo-European language. It belongs to a wide family of languages spoken across Europe and as far east as India that trace their origins back over 4,500 years. Irish belongs to the Celtic branch of the Indo-European family; it and three other members of this branch—Scottish Gaelic, Welsh, and Breton—are today alive as community languages.

The form of Celtic from which Irish descended, Goedelic, was brought to Ireland by the invading Celts around 300 B.C., according to some scholars. (We know nothing of the languages of the pre-Celtic people who inhabited the island for six thousand years before the coming of the Celts.)

The Celts emerged as a culturally distinct people in central Europe more than a thousand years before Christ and spread their power and speech over all of Europe and parts of Asia. Other Celtic languages were Gaulish, which died out at the beginning of the Christian era, and British, from which Welsh, Cornish, and Breton are descended.

In the fifth century, Christianity was brought to Ireland and with it came the art of writing and the Latin alphabet. Later in the same century, invaders from northeastern Ireland brought the Irish language to Scotland, where it gradually spread over all the country.

In Ireland the Irish language can be seen to go through four stages of continuous historical development, as far as the written form is concerned: Old Irish (600–900 A.D.), Middle Irish (900–1200 A.D.), Early Modern (or Classical) Irish (1200–1650 A.D.), and Modern Irish.

Throughout this development Irish borrowed words from other languages, especially Latin, Norse, Anglo-Norman (a dialect of French), and English.

Old Irish is the oldest form of the language of which records survive. A considerable body of literature from this period remains, and Irish has the oldest vernacular literature in Europe after Greek and Latin. It was a period of standardization imposed by a small learned class who were based mainly in the monasteries. Many words were borrowed from Latin during this period, especially words relating to learning and religion.

The Middle Irish period saw the breaking down of the Old Irish system to be replaced by a less rigid form of the language. The language of this period represents the struggle between the evolving speech of the people and the older standard upheld by the scholars. Many words of Norse origin entered the Irish language at this period and later, the Anglo-Norman impact on Irish society was reflected in the great number of Anglo-Norman words that entered the language.

In the Early Modern Irish period, a new literary form was cultivated in the Bardic Schools, in which learned laymen were given patronage for writing poems in praise of the aristocracy. With the collapse of the Irish aristocracy after the battle of Kinsale in 1601, the Bardic Schools came to an end. The Classical language began to decay and a new literary tradition took its place.

In 1600 Irish was the language of the whole country outside Dublin and a few other English settlements. Two hundred and fifty-one years later, when the first census to include language returns was taken, three years after the Great Famine (1845–1848), Irish was spoken by only a million and a half people who made up twenty-three percent of the population. In 1871 this group numbered less than a million.

A movement to restore Irish emerged at the end of the nineteenth century that was later to play an important part in the struggle for national independence. Since independence in 1922, it has been the official policy of the native government, in name at least, to preserve the Gaeltacht and to restore the Irish language. The 1937 Constitution states that Irish is the first official language, but nearly all central and local government business is conducted in English. Although successive surveys have shown that the majority of the Irish people wish to see the Irish language restored, the effort necessary to fulfill that wish seems to be missing. A positive sign in recent years has been the setting up of an Irish language radio station, Raidió na Gaeltachta, in 1972, and the growing demand by parents all over the country for more Irish-medium schooling for their children.

IRELAND OF THE PROVERB

Introductory Proverbs

Ní hé lá na gaoithe lá na scolb.

The windy day is not the day for scollops (thatching).

Scollops are slender rods of willow, hazel, or briers, or slips of bog deal, for pinning the thatch to the roof underneath. To thatch a new house a layer of grass sod, cut from the surface of the ground, is laid upon the roof timbers, and the straw is then secured to the sod.

The Irish traditional thatched house, to many people, has almost become a symbol of national identity. Although modern bungalows have replaced most of our thatched houses, there are still enough of them left to remind us of our past and of a way of life that is fast disappearing. Traditional houses as we know them today probably date back to the seventeenth century, but thatch dates back to our earliest inhabitants.

Although our thatched houses are favorite photographic subjects for tourists, certain photographs from the past can evoke unpleasant memories. Eviction scenes from less than a century ago, with the thatch on fire and the dreaded battering ram at work knocking down the walls, are frightening reminders of our troubled history. Our ballads remind us that the pikes forged and used during the 1798 rebellion were often hidden in the thatch. My own most abiding memory of thatch, however, is the recollection of myself as a child in my native Connemara catching the wren ("The King of All Birds") in the thatch, in the late evening of Christmas Day, to bring it proudly in the jam jar from house to house on Saint Stephen's Day—The Wren Day (*Lá an Dreoilín*). Happily, the custom is still alive, though it is not as vibrant as it used to be.

As the proverb suggests, wind is the natural enemy of thatch. The Night of the Big Wind, the night of January 6, 1839, is still vivid in folk memory. A hurricane hit the country and thatched roofs were shredded by the wind and set alight by the flying embers from the hearths. When the Old Age Pension Scheme was introduced seventy years later, in 1909, a memory of The Night of the Big Wind was sufficient evidence that the person was old enough to qualify.

Thatching, Crossmolina, Co. Mayo.

Thatched cottage, Carraroe, Connemara, Co. Galway.

Ar scáth a chéile a mhaireas na daoine.

People live in one another's shelter.

The Irish word *scáth*, which I have translated "shelter," has many meanings. It can mean a shadow, a shade, darkness; a screen, a curtain; a veil, cover, defense, protection; pretence, pretext; sake (in "for the sake of"); good (in "for the good of"); even bashfulness, fear, or nervousness.

A group of neighbors, helping a farmer to save the turf or hay, or to finish some other work on the farm before the good weather broke, was called a *meitheal*. This group of helping neighbors usually included the farmer's brothers or cousins, or other members of the extended family. "A little relationship is worth a lot of charity" (*Is fearr beagán den ghaol ná mórán den charthanas*) says another Irish proverb, and the first aspect of family connection was the duty of material help. *Comhar na gComharsan* (cooperation of neighbors) was a much-used phrase and a much-practiced act.

Side by side with the modern methods, turf (peat) is still being harvested in the traditional way all over Ireland. It is cut by a "slane" (a special spade) into long sods which are left to dry on the turf-bank. To hasten the drying process, the sods are turned and "footed" (stood against each other), and when they are dry they are brought home to be used as fuel for cooking and heating.

Peat bogs cover almost a sixth of the land surface of Ireland, and Bord na Móna, the Irish Peat Development Authority, since its inception in 1946, has very successfully harnessed modern technology to exploit this resource.

The top layer of many Irish bogs consists mainly of sphagnum moss, a light, fibrous substance that has little use as a fuel. However, its spongy texture makes it an excellent soil conditioner, adding body to light soils or porosity to heavy ones. In contrast to fuel peat, which is sold entirely within Ireland, ninety percent of horticultural peat processed in Ireland is marketed worldwide under the now familiar brand name of Shamrock Irish Moss Peat.

There is, however, the growing danger that we would allow all our bogland to be converted into fuel or moss, thereby destroying a vast variety of our unique flora and fauna.

Turf cutting in Ballyferriter, Co. Kerry, in 1946.

4

Bringing home the turf, Gorumna Island, Connemara, Co. Galway.

Ní dhéanfadh an domhan capall rása d'asal.

The world would not make a racehorse of a donkey.

To be compared to a donkey can be very insulting. This is so in spite of, or perhaps because of, the fact that the donkey was the animal most widely used as a beast of burden in Ireland until quite recently. Donkeys or asses were used to carry loads on their backs during the Napoleonic wars in Europe, when horses were in great demand for the war campaigns. They were known in Ireland long before that, however, and their bones have been excavated from a site in Co. Fermanagh that dates back to before 1400 B.C.

Generations of Irish children have been told that the cross on the donkey's back is a reminder that there was a donkey in the stable in Bethlehem when Jesus was born there, that a donkey carried Jesus and Mary on the Flight into Egypt, and that Jesus, many years later, rode into Jerusalem on the back of a donkey. This makes it all the more difficult to explain how an animal, which has served rural Ireland so well, should be for centuries the emblem of stupidity and the object of ridicule. The most common reference to the cross on the donkey's back nowadays is that a habitual drunkard could drink it off: "He could drink the cross off the donkey" (*D'ólfadh sé an chros den asal*), or that a notorious thief would steal it.

In certain areas, however, the donkey was respectfully referred to as "My Saviour's horse" (*Capall mo Shlánaitheora*), and a white donkey's milk was believed to be a cure for whooping cough.

The most common way of carrying a load on a donkey's back was in pairs of baskets (also called paniers, creels, or *pardógs*) suspended on either side of a wooden pack saddle, which sits on a mat of braided straw. The baskets were nearly always made of sally rods, and some of them had collapsible bottoms to facilitate unloading. The donkey and baskets were most commonly used to carry turf (peat) from the bog, manure onto the land, or seaweed from the seashore. Water was carried in specially made stave-built containers, and similar containers were probably used in the eighteenth and nineteenth centuries to transport butter from all parts of Munster to the great butter market in Cork.

Donkey and wooden plough, Gweedone (Gaoth Dobhair), Co. Donegal.

Níl aon tinteán mar do thinteán féin.

There is no fireside like your own fireside.

On the face of it, this looks like "There's no place like home," but there is more to it than that. Your own fireside meant your own house and land, and the proverb expresses the desire of the parents of old to have their daughter married, where she would be mistress of her own house, instead of having to go into domestic service in a nearby town or city. Even then, farmers had to divide what little land they had between their sons and sell what they could in order to provide dowries for their daughters.

If a daughter did not get married in her late teens, the best strategy was for her to go to the United States, if an older sister or an aunt there would send the passage. While in domestic service in Boston, New York, or Chicago, she would become expert in the various skills of good housekeeping, and when she would come home on holidays in five years' time she could have her choice of husband.

The very word "fireside" still conveys the idea of warmth, comfort, and hospitality. The hearth was the focal point in every house, and in drafty houses the only truly warm place was near the fire. It was there that the family's meals were cooked and often eaten, and the turf-fire in the evenings was the principal source of light.

The settle bed in the corner could be used as a seat during the day and as a bed at night, and the feather mattress for this bed was usually made and brought into the house by the young bride.

The house in the photograph is on the Middle Island of the Aran Islands in Galway Bay. As there is no peat on the islands, the inhabitants of old dried cow dung and burned it as fuel, and this is still the custom in India and in many other parts of the world. To supplement this fuel, the Aran Islanders, until recently, depended on peat brought across from the mainland in the now world-famous Connemara turf-boats called Galway Hookers.

Fireside in a house on Inishmaan, Aran Islands.

Ní gabháil go lánseol agus ní balla go huillinn.

You are not a fully fledged sailor unless you have sailed under full sail, and you have not built a wall unless you rounded a corner.

This proverb is a reminder of the versatility of our ancestors. Not only could they handle a boat under full sail, but some of them built their own boats and sailed them as far as America. The Connemara *Bád Mór* (Big Boat), commonly known as the Galway Hooker, is the last Irish working sail craft left. For centuries these boats have been used in Galway Bay both for fishing and ferrying. They brought turf and livestock from Connemara to the Aran Islands and to other parts of counties Galway and Clare, and they brought timber and provisions from Galway to the boatwrights and shopkeepers of Connemara. With the improvement of roads and the coming of the truck in the thirties and forties of this century, these fine boats were allowed to rot in the small Connemara harbors until a restoration movement in the seventies and eighties was successful in saving them from virtual extinction.

The Galway Hooker in the photograph is the forty-foot *Saint Patrick*, built by the famous Casey family in Mweenish (Muínis) in Connemara in 1911. Known as *Bád Chonroy (Conroy's Boat)*, it was owned by a shopkeeper, P. D. Conroy, and for years brought general provisions from Galway to Ros Muc in the Connemara heartland. On July 4, 1986, the present owner, Paddy Barry, and his crew of five, cruised past the Statue of Liberty in New York Harbor, af-ter sailing five thousand miles across the Atlantic. It was the first Galway Hooker ever to have done so.

The *Saint Patrick* was not, however, the first Galway-built boat to sail to America. Anthony Conneely (Toona Ó Conaola) from Lettermullen in Connemara, at the beginning of the nineteenth century, built an eighty-foot brig, sailed it on its maiden voyage to Saint John's, New Brunswick, on the east coast of Canada, and brought a load of timber home to Galway in it. The boat was known as the *Brig Saint John* and on October 7, 1849, under Captain Oliver from Claddagh in Galway (home of the Claddagh Ring), it foundered in a gale off the shore of Cohasset, outside Boston. Of the 121 people on board, fleeing from the horrors of the Great Famine in Ireland, only twenty-two survived.

The Galway Hooker, Saint Patrick.

The Saint Patrick *in Boston, July 1986.*

Ní neart go cur le chéile.

There is not strength without unity.

Nowhere is this proverb more apt than in the case of fishermen on the western coast of Ireland who still use the round-bottomed, keelless craft known as the "currach." The history of the currach is as old as the history of Ireland itself. Formerly covered with animal skins, usually cowhides, the covering nowadays is of tarred canvas, over a frame of wooden laths. The currach gives easily in broken water and will survive the most violent sea. It is, of course, very vulnerable, and the least touch of a sharp rock or a drifting spar can put a hole in it. It is of the utmost importance that the crew of three or four oarsmen rows in unison. This is the origin of the common expression in Irish, *"Caithfidh tú tarraingt le foireann"* (You will have to pull [row] with the crew), to remind people that they have to get on with others.

Although part-time fishing is still a very important part of the year's work for small farmers in the coastal regions, many of the wide variety of traditional methods have now largely disappeared. Line fishing from currachs and small wooden boats, using spillers (long trawl lines, carrying many hooks) is now a thing of the past, and seine netting, which was popular in large estuaries and along the coast, is no longer practiced. For hundreds of years the basking shark (*liamhán gréine*) was fished commercially off the western coast of Ireland, and Robert Flaherty's film, *Man of Aran*, captured some of the excitement and danger experienced by our forefathers in hunting the basking shark.

Launching a boat, Mulrany, Co. Mayo.

Carrying the currach on Inishmaan (Inis Meáin, Middle Island), Aran Islands.

14

Ní heolas go haontíos.

You must live with a person to know a person.

"If you want to know me come and live with me."

This proverb is often quoted in regard to marriage, although, of course, it has a much wider meaning. Arranged or matchmade marriages were common in rural Ireland, and the reaction of young men and women who objected to matchmaking often resulted in the "runaway" marriage. Whether they married for love or for land, which was not unheard of, the young couple, then as now, had to settle down together and get to know one another.

On small holdings in the west of Ireland, the women worked on the farm in addition to doing all the housekeeping, as the men hardly ever did any of the domestic work. Only in exceptional cases did a woman do heavy work such as reaping with a scythe, cutting turf with a slane, rowing a boat, or cutting seaweed, but she carried more loads on her back than did her husband.

Hugh Brody writes in *Inishkillane:*

At marriage the bride moved to the groom's family home, taking nothing with her. Dowries were given by a girl's father to her new husband. The new wife owned not so much as a teacup. And she owned no more when she was eighty: everything passed to her son, whose wife in her turn would use but never own the household possessions. Women were also excluded from the social centres of the community: they never went to the bars, rarely exchanged visits, and only when they had reached old age was the wisdom attributed to years allowed to transcend, in public life, the insignificance attributed to womanhood. In home and community life alike, therefore, the woman's influence may have been significant, but it was informal and domestic: women had at least to appear to be without authority just as they were in practice without possessions.

Married couple in traditional dress, Connemara, Co. Galway.

Bíonn dhá insint ar scéal agus dhá leagan déag ar amhrán.

There are two sides to every story and twelve versions of a song.

"There are two sides to every story."

Storytelling and traditional singing were two of the principal forms of entertainment for the people of rural Ireland in the past. The art of storytelling still survives, but it is now confined mainly to a small band of people who very often only tell the stories for the sake of having them recorded. At least forty-three thousand versions of seven hundred different international "tale types" have been recorded in Ireland, according to S. Ó Súilleabháin and R. Th. Christiansen in *The Types of Irish Folktale*. Stories were originally told in the Irish language, and the Irish-speaking districts produced some of the richest material.

Carna in South Connemara is still well known for its wealth of traditional songs and stories, and it was in this area that the late Séamus Ennis recorded 212 songs from one man in the early nineteen forties.

This wealth of songs and stories survived through the centuries, as indeed did the folk music and dance of the people. In the country houses storytelling, singing, music, and dancing brought gaiety to people whose lives were often deprived of material comforts. It was these aspects of life and tradition that made so many Irish emigrants remember their homeland with such affection, and some of the finest early collections of Irish music were made by emigrants in America.

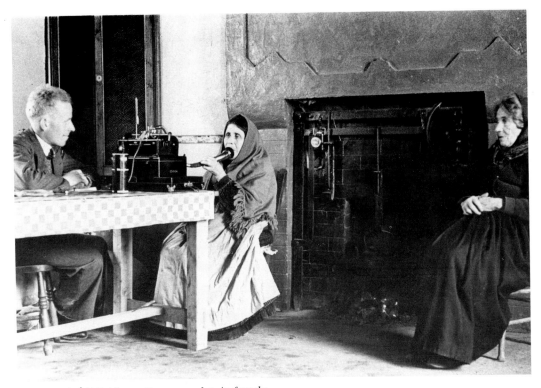

*Dr. Seosamh Ó Dálaigh recording songs and stories from the
late Cáit and Máire Ruiséal, in Dunquin, Co. Kerry, 1942.*

Béarfaidh bó éigin lao éigin lá éigin.

Some cow will give birth to some calf some day.

The optimist who first said these hopeful words knew full well that the cow has always been a source of food and wealth in rural Ireland. Cows are known to have existed in Ireland since Neolithic times (4000–2000 B.C.). Only the small breed of Kerry cows remains of the pre-medieval Irish cattle types, and there are not many of them left in the country now.

Irish society in the medieval period (mid-twelfth to mid-sixteenth centuries) was based more on pastoralism than on agriculture, and stock raising was more important than tillage. The care of cattle was the concern of the whole family, and cattle raiding was an enduring aspect of rural society in the seventeenth century. The early Irish epic poems describe these raids, and annals record occasions when a thousand animals were captured in a single raid. *The Cattle Raid of Cooley (Táin Bó Cuailnge)* is one of our best-known mythological sagas. To understand this society it is necessary to compare it with the pastoral societies that have survived into modern times, mainly in Third World countries.

An interesting aspect of pastoral life in Ireland that survived into the present century was the removal of some herds to summer pastures in the hills. From May to October, all the girls in a village would take the cows to the hill pastures, where the village men had earlier built huts, usually of sod, in a dry spot near a stream. These huts were the girls' homes for the summer months while they made butter, carded wool, and knitted socks. Although they worked hard, there was time for merrymaking, and occasional nights of singing and dancing took place when the boys from the village visited. This custom of transhumance was well known in Europe, and there is widespread evidence that it was common in many parts of Ireland. The remains of the "booley huts," as they were called (*buaile*), can still be found on many Irish hillsides.

Bringing home the cows.

Bíonn súil le muir ach ní bhíonn súil le tír.

There is hope from the sea but there is no hope from the land (grave).

It is not surprising that a community of coastal fishermen, comprised largely of nonswimmers, should have superstitions about the sea. Although many a fisherman was lost at sea, it was not until the body or boat was found that all hope was abandoned. There have been many remarkable instances of fishermen, caught in a gale and given up for dead, who sailed or rowed safely home several days later.

Although there was a certain inevitability about drowning, families suffered untold grief when the bodies of their dear ones were never recovered. John Millington Synge immortalized this grief in his play, *Riders to the Sea*, in which Maurya, an old Aran Island woman, laments the recent drowning of her youngest son, Bartley, and the previous drowning of her husband and five other sons:

Bartley will be lost now, and let you call in Éamon and make me a good coffin out of the white boards for I won't live after them. I've had a husband and a husband's father, and six sons in this house—six fine men, though it was a hard birth I had with every one of them and they coming to the world—and some of them were found and some of them were not found, but they're gone now the lot of them. . . .
There were Stephen and Shawn were lost in the great wind, and found after in the Bay of Gregory of the Golden Mouth, and carried up, the two of them, on one plank, and in by that door. . . . There was Sheamus and his father, and his own father again, were lost in a dark night, and not a stick or sign was seen of them when the sun went up. There was Patch after was drowned out of a currach that turned over. . . . They're all gone now and there isn't anything more the sea can do to me.

Funeral on Inisheer (Inis Oírr), Aran Islands.

21

Great Blasket Island (An Blascaod Mór), Co. Kerry.

Youth and Age
Óige agus Aois

Peig Sayers (1873–1958) is one of three authors from the Great Blasket Island (An Blascaod Mór), off Kerry, each of whom produced a remarkable autobiographical book at the beginning of this century. Her book is simply called *Peig;* the other two are *An tOileánach (The Islandman)* by Tomás Ó Criomhthain, and *Fiche Bliain ag Fás (Twenty Years A-Growing)* by Muiris Ó Súilleabháin. All three books have been translated into English and have become bestsellers.

Another one of Peig Sayers's books, *Machtnamh Seana-Mhná (An Old Woman's Reflections)*, has been mentioned in the introduction to this book because of the unusually large number of proverbs contained in it. The title of the first chapter of the book is a proverb, "Pity How Youth Goes" (*Trua Mar Imíos an Óige*), and in this chapter Peig says:

Youth slips away as the water slips away from the sand of the shore. A person falls into age unknown to himself. I think there are no two jewels more valuable than Youth and Health. Here am I now, doubled up with age, on a green sward beside the house, reflecting and musing on the days of my youth. Och! Wasn't it I was agile and light then! Small thought I had that I'd ever be a worn old one like this! On that fine harvest evening long ago, coming from Dingle, when I sat on the Jackdaw's Rock to rest, and looking around me and west at the islands, little did I think that 'twas on that Big Island I'd have to spend my life!

In the last chapter Peig continues:

My spell on this little green sward is nearly finished. It's sad and low and lonely I am to be parting with it. *Long as the day is, night comes,* and alas, night is coming for me, too. I am parting with you, my beautiful little grassy plot, sun of my life. Other people will have your pleasure in future, but I'll be far away from you in a kingdom I don't know. . . . My blessing and the blessing of God be with Youth.

Peig Sayers found comfort in the thought that her books would be read long after her death and found, once more, support in the great store of her beloved proverbs:

Is buaine port ná glór na n-éan
Is buaine focal ná toice an tsaoil.

A tune is more lasting than the song of the birds,
And a word more lasting than the wealth of the world.

Peig Sayers in 1946.

23

Mol an óige agus tiocfaidh sí.

Praise the young and they will blossom.

The present generation of rural Irish children is luckier than previous ones in that they live in an era when they hear words of praise and encouragement from parents, teachers, priests, and leaders of society. In the Ireland of the past, I think it can be truthfully said that the above proverb was more widely quoted than it was abided by.

Another proverb that was quoted too often to children was "Sweet is the sound of the silent mouth" (*Is binn béal ina thost*), and they were continually reminded that little ones should be seen and not heard. Children were too often afraid to open their mouths in the presence of adults, and the element of fear loomed large in their lives. They were afraid of their teachers, some of whom in excessive diligence, and others is sheer bad temper, exercised corporal punishment much too liberally. For the children to complain to their parents would only insure a repetition of the chastisement at home.

Many priests in rural Ireland were not noted for their kindness to children either, and the fact that schoolchildren were constantly slapped at school for failing to memorize long and difficult catechism answers did not endear the teachers or priests to Irish youth. The *garda*, or policeman, was looked upon more as a threat than as a protecive force. All in all, many of the rural Irish youth of previous generations did not sense much freedom until they took the emigrant ship and found themselves in an alien, but very often a more open, society.

Some parish priests declared open war on young courting couples, and it was not unusual for such priests, armed with a heavy stick, to roam the roads at night putting young Irish men and women to flight. It was a very paternalistic society and emigrant Irish people who experienced it will be glad to hear that a more relaxed and tolerant relationship has developed between the generations during the past quarter century or so.

Children running to their grandmother, Connemara, Co. Galway.

Is minic a rinne bromach gioblach capall cumasach.

A raggy colt often made a powerful horse.

The Connemara pony, probably the only breed of Irish horse that can claim to be indigenous, has greatly increased in popularity in recent years. It is a hardy breed with a healthy constitution that makes it adaptable to almost any climate. Connemara ponies have been sent to India, California, Sweden, British Columbia, Italy, Denmark, Britain, and France, and they are now being bred in countries outside Ireland.

One of our exported ponies, Marconi, won the Championship Stallion Class of the United States in 1963, and his son, El Gotto, won the Green Hunter Championship against full-sized American show-jumpers at the 1966 Washington International Horse Show. Tommy Wade's Dundrum won the King George V Gold Cup in London, and has, on two occasions, been instrumental in Ireland's winning the Aga Khan Cup in Dublin. An overgrown specimen, about fifteen hands (sixty inches high), he has cleared seven feet two inches. In the field of dressage the Connemara pony Little Model has competed all over Europe and has won the British Championship nine times in eleven years.

The Connemara Pony Society was founded in 1923 when it started its first stud book to standardize the breed. Heights range from thirteen to fourteen and one-half hands when registered at the age of two years, but most ponies grow taller afterwards. Their coats are gray, dun, cream, bay, brown, black, and occasionally roan or chestnut. Piebalds and skewbalds or ponies with broken colors are not acceptable for registration.

The annual Connemara Pony Show, held in Clifden in Connemara every August, attracts buyers from all the world and many more go there for the sheer pleasure of viewing the fine collection of Connemara ponies.

A Connemara pony.

26

Young man with pony in Ballyconneely, Co. Galway.

Tá onóir ag an aois agus uaisle ag an óige.

Age is honorable and youth is noble.

Age and youth, Casla, Connemara.

Is iomaí craiceann a chuireas an óige di.

Youth sheds many a skin.

Dublin youths.

Ní mhaireann rith maith ag an each i gcónaí.

The steed does not retain its speed forever.

The breeding of good horses is one of Ireland's outstanding accomplishments. This applies to almost every category of horse: thoroughbred, steeplechaser, point-to-pointer, hunter, Olympic three day event horse, show-jumper, dressage performer, Connemara pony, and others. Credit should be given, however, to the source from which most of these horses derive their outstanding qualities—the Irish farm mare. Our method of "outcross" breeding is almost unique, in that we cross thoroughbred sires with Irish draft mares. Our famous Irish

Old man, The Liberties, Dublin.

On the road near Ardgroom, Beara Peninsula, Co. Cork.

horses may boast descent from exotic thoroughbred sires for three or four generations, but it is the Irish farm mare that gives them the bone, substance, and stamina.

In show-jumping, the success of Irish horses has been remarkable in partnership with both Irish and foreign riders. The world's leading equestrian authority, the *Fédération Équestre Internationale*, stated that between 1918 and 1939 the world's three best show-jumpers were the Irish Army's Blarney Castle, Limerick Lace, and Red Hugh. Since then, Irish-breds have registered countless show-jumping successes, both in individual and team competitions.

Ireland won the Aga Khan Cup at the Dublin Horse Show three years in a row, in 1977, 1978, and 1979, and again in 1984 and 1987.

Ireland has many advantages as a horse-breeding country. The mild climate permits young stock to live outdoors nearly all year round, giving them a hardy constitution from foalhood. The limestone soil in most of the better breeding localities supplies the calcium so essential for sturdy bone formation. Large stud-farms concentrate on thoroughbred racehorses, but many of the excellent thoroughbreds are the products of small farms.

Horse and round tower, Kilmacduagh, Co. Galway.

Tús agus deireadh an duine tarraingt ar an tine.

The beginning and end of one's life is to draw closer to the fire.

This proverb reflects the timeless observation that young children are fascinated by fire, and old people draw near the fire in order to keep warm. In all Irish country houses, the fire was the center of activity and the most important part of the house. When times were hard and turf (peat) was scarce, it was difficult for people to cook or to keep warm, but after a good dry summer there was usually plenty of turf and a roaring fire on the hearth.

The grandmother and grandfather had an accepted place in the house. They usually sat by the fire, and part of their duty was to make sure that none of the younger children, for whom the fire held such a fascination, ventured too near the hot ashes. The grandparents' accumulated knowledge and wisdom was respected and often called upon, and they did their share of the housework and child-minding. They often recited tales and poems for the household's entertainment in the long winter evenings and, no doubt, passed on many a proverb and many a song to their grandchildren.

The house in rural Ireland served as a workshop for various occupations. Most houses had all the tools necessary for converting the sheep's fleece into woolen thread, and for converting the wheat, oats, or barley into ground meal.

Fireside scene, Casla, Connemara, Co. Galway.

Man and spinning wheel, Glencolumbkille, Co. Donegal.

An tslat nuair a chríonas le haois, is deacair í a shníomh ina gad.

The (sally) rod, when it withers with age, is difficult to weave into a withe.

There are many variations of this proverb, both in Ireland and in Scotland, including: "When the twig grows hard it's difficult to twist it," "Bend the sapling while it is young," "The crook in the old stick is hard to take out."

At one time in Ireland sally (willow) gardens were as plentiful as fields of potatoes, and sally rods were used to make paniers (creels) for horses and donkeys, as well as for a wide variety of household containers. Perhaps the most common of these was the round, shallow, basin-like container called the *ciseog*. It was also called a "teeming basket," as the potatoes were strained in it. It was then placed on top of the pot in the middle of the floor while the family sat round it to eat the potatoes.

The sally was planted in springtime, and the planting simply involved pushing cuttings of twenty-five to thirty centimeters (ten to twelve inches) well into the soil. As sally grows easily, it needs little attention other than careful and frequent weeding during the first two seasons and annual cutting of the most tender shoots to promote fresh growth. It was usually harvested in the winter months and stored in bundles in an outhouse to dry.

To make a creel, pointed sally rods, about

Making sally baskets, Co. Donegal.

three hundred centimeters in height, are driven into the ground. Slightly thicker rods are woven between the upright rods at ground level in order to make a strong rimwale (*buinne béil*), and more slender rods are used for the rest of the weave. To complete the bottom of the creel, the upright rods are bent over and interwoven in groups of four. When the bottom has been completed, the creel can be pulled from the ground.

Mweenish (Muínis), Connemara, Co. Galway.

35

Ní thagann an óige faoi dhó choíche ach tagann an brón faoi dhó san oíche.

Youth never comes twice but sorrow comes twice a night.

An old person whose friends and contemporaries are all dead is often referred to as Oisín after the Fianna (*Oisín i ndiaidh na Féinne*). The Fianna were a mythical band of warriors who were supposed to have lived in Ireland before the coming of Christianity. Their leader was Finn Mac Cool (Fionn Mac Cumhaill), and Oisín was his son. One morning while hunting near the lakes of Killarney, they were approached by a beautiful, golden-haired young woman riding on a large white steed. She told them she was Niamh of the Golden Hair (Niamh Chinn Óir), and that she came from the Land of Youth (*Tír na nÓg*) because she was in love with Oisín. She wanted him to go with her to the Land of Youth, where everyone is forever young, and Oisín, having fallen instantly in love with her, jumped up on the horse behind her, and off they went over the western ocean to the Land of Youth.

Before he left, he promised Fionn and the Fianna that he would come back to visit them in three years' time. Niamh gave him the white steed to take him back, but she warned him that if his feet touched the land of Ireland, he would never more return. In a quiet glen called Glenasmole (Gleann na Smól, Valley of Thrushes), near where Dublin now stands, he came upon a group of men trying to move a big stone in a field. As he bent down to give them a hand, the girth of the saddle broke and Oisín fell to the ground. On touching the land of Ireland, he was transformed into a withered old man with long white hair. The white steed turned away and galloped toward the west. What Oisín had thought to have been three years were in fact three hundred years. He told them he was Oisín, son of Fionn Mac Cumhaill, and they brought him to meet St. Patrick who had just come to Ireland.

Old age, Dublin.

Bíonn gach tosach lag.

Every beginning is weak.

Twin foals, Connemara, Co. Galway.

Walkers, Glanmore Lake,
Co. Cork.

Is cuma leis an óige cá leagann sí a cos.

Youth does not mind where it sets its foot.

The Great Blasket Island (An Blascaod Mór).

Death

An Bás

The Blasket Island (An Blascaod), off Kerry, until its inhabitants moved to the mainland in Dunquin (Dún Chaoin) in 1953, was known as "the next parish to America," it being the most westerly parish in Ireland. From the beginning of this century this Irish-speaking island community was visited by a group of foreign Celtic scholars, whose fusion with the island people resulted in a considerable corpus of island literature, both in Irish and in English.

One of these scholars was an Englishman named Robin Flower (1881–1946), who wrote *The Western Island*, a truly beautiful account of the Blasket people, their traditional tales, folklore, and songs. In his preface to this book, Robin Flower refers to the vast number of proverbs they had on the subject of death:

On one of my visits after a long interval I remember how, on the evening of my return, a number of my friends had gathered in one of the houses to bid me welcome. In the course of our talk we began to reckon up the deaths which had occurred since my last visit. The talk inevitably took the form of a recitation of the rich store of proverbs accumulated in a folk civilization on the necessity of death and the consolations of religious faith. One by one, almost as though reciting a liturgy, men and women produced each one his or her contribution from that apparently inexhaustible supply. At last, however, a silence fell as they waited, visibly searching their minds for a fresh inspiration. Suddenly an old woman in the corner leaned forward and said with an air of finality, *"Cá bhfuil an sneachta a bhí chomh geal anuraidh?"* (Where is the snow that was so bright last year?). I sprang up in excitement and cried out: *"Où sont les neiges d'antan?"* (Where are the snows of yesteryear?). "Who said that?" asked the King, an expert in this lore. "Francois Villon said it," I replied. "And who was he?" he returned. "Was he a Connaughtman?" "No, he lived hundreds of years ago and he said it in French, and it was a proverb of his people." "Well," broke in Tomás, "you can't better the proverb. I've always heard that the French are a clever people, and I wouldn't put it past them to have said that before we did."

When Robin Flower wrote these words in 1944, the custom of waking the dead was very much alive on the Great Blasket Island and all over the mainland. The waking of the dead is a very ancient custom throughout the world, and we have accounts of wakes in Europe going back almost a thousand years. With the following proverbs on Death, a short account is given of present-day wakes and the wakes of centuries gone by.

Caherciveen, Co. Kerry.

Nuair a thiocfas an bás ní imeoidh sé folamh.

When death comes it will not go away empty.

In some island communities and in remote country places, the tradition of burying the dead in plain white homemade coffins still exists. The ancient custom of waking the dead still survives in parts of Ireland, although it died out during the past century on most of the continent of Europe. The wakes of today, however, are very different from the wakes of old, which were very often happy social functions with merriment and games.

When somebody dies in rural Ireland nowadays and it is decided to wake the body in the house (a custom that has died out in most places), someone is immediately sent for provisions of food and drink for the wake. The corpse is usually laid out by neighboring women. They wash the body, put a habit on it, and prepare the bed or table on which the corpse will be placed. A crucifix is laid on the breast, and rosary beads are entwined in the fingers. White sheets are hung over the bed or table, and candles are lit near the remains.

The immediate relatives then approach the corpse and express their grief, in either muffled sobs or loud wailing or "keening." ("Keen" comes from the Irish word *caoin*, to cry.) Neighbors come in and express their sympathy ("I am sorry for your trouble" is the usual expression), pray for the dead person, and then retreat to make room for others. Custom demands that the corpse must not be left unattended for the duration of the wake before being brought to the church on the evening before the burial. The wake-house is visited during the day mainly by elderly people, and at nightfall the neighbors and parishioners generally go to pay their respects. All are given drink and food, tobacco or snuff. The Rosary is recited once or twice during the night, around midnight and again toward morning. Most of the parishioners leave around midnight, and the near neighbors and relatives stay up all night waking the dead.

Carrying the coffin on Inishmaan, Aran Islands.

Connemara, Co. Galway.

Bíonn an bás ar aghaidh an tseanduine agus ar chúl an duine óig.

Death is in front of the old person and at the back of the young person.

Some of the best traditional songs in Irish are laments for a spouse or a loved one who died at a young age. Many of them are about drowning tragedies, like the lament for Liam Ó Raghallaigh (Liam O'Reilly) which expresses the grief of a young woman whose husband was drowned on their wedding day. The accident happened in northwest Mayo nearly two hundred years ago as the groom was sailing home to his bride, having delivered the elderly priest who officiated at the wedding to his home across the bay. The following verses are from a lament taken from *Blas Meala (A Sip from the Honey Pot)*, a collection of Gaelic folk songs with English translations by Brian O'Rourke:

Will ye not weep for my great sorrow? for I'm a
    widow and still a maid,
And my husband of a morning is tossed and
    rolling upon the waves;
Had I been in the boat that evening holding
    fiercely on to the sail,
I swear on the Bible, Liam O'Reilly, I'd have
    saved you from your fate.

'Tis no wonder they say of your father the heart
    inside him has turned to lead,
And likewise your white-haired mother on
    whose white milk you once were fed,
Not to mention the girl you married, who never
    managed to share your bed,
For when my arms should have been around
    you, oh, you were drowned and lying dead.

Oh, the crabs have devoured your mouth, love,
    the eels have feasted upon your eyes,
And your white hands so strong and tender are
    now the salmon's proudest prize;
I'd pay a fortune to any boatman who'd show
    me where your body lies,
And ease the burden of Nellie Jordan, who'll
    get no rest till the day she dies.

Ní huasal ná íseal ach thuas seal agus thíos seal.

It is not a matter of upper or lower class but of being up a while and down a while.

Gravedigger, Caherciveen, Co. Kerry.

Síleann do chara agus do namhaid nach bhfaighidh tú bás choíche.

Both your friend and your enemy think that you will never die.

Drumcliff, Co. Sligo, where the poet W. B. Yeats is buried.

Is minic a ligeas béal na huaighe rud chuig béal na truaighe.

The mouth of the grave often allows something to go to the mouth of the poor.

If the purpose of the wake nowadays is to pray for the dead person and to sympathize with the relatives, it had a much different purpose in days gone by. More alcohol was consumed at the wakes long ago, usually whiskey or poteen (*poitín*), and the playing of games and unruly behavior often reached unseemly proportions.

In 1778 Thomas Campbell described the wakes that he saw in Ireland as occasions for merriment and feasting, where people assembled from far and near; the grown-ups among them passed the time by smoking and drinking whiskey—so much, Campbell thought, that the relatives of the deceased would be impoverished forever after.

Storytelling was very common at wakes all over Ireland, and singing at wakes was widespread in Ireland and abroad. There are still many Irish who have heard singing at wakes or have sung at them themselves, but the custom has now died out almost everywhere. Dancing, too, was a usual feature of Irish wakes during the past three centuries at least, and various efforts were made by some of the Irish bishops to end the custom. It is said that even the corpse was sometimes taken out to dance! Accounts of wakes in neighboring Scotland tell that the dancing was led by the relatives of the deceased.

Cards were sometimes played at wakes, and if it happened that the dead person had been fond of cards, the friends sat around the bed, and a hand of cards was even given to the corpse. Riddles and tongue twisters provided much merriment, and Seán Ó Súilleabháin has devoted a full chapter to the games played at wakes in his book, *Irish Wake Amusements*.

Maoras Cemetery, Baile na hAbhann, Connemara, Co. Galway.

Is beag an rud is buaine ná an duine.

The smallest of things outlives the human being.

This is a reminder of the transience of life, and the continuing existence of the proverb is ample vindication of its simple message. Whichever woman or man first said it is long since dead, but the saying will be repeated as long as there is somebody left to do so.

Our ancient ancestors left behind them things that not only outlived them but will also outlive generations to come. It is thought that the first settlers, primitive hunters, came to Ireland around 6000 B.C., and that the first farming colonists, who raised animals and cultivated the soil,

Newgrange, Co. Meath.

reached our shores around 3000 B.C. It was this latter civilization that left us the large stone tombs we now call "court cairns," "portal graves" (dolmens), and "passage graves." Three of these five-thousand-year-old passage graves, Newgrange, Dowth, and Knowth, lie only a short distance from Dublin, in the Boyne Valley near Drogheda. Of the three, only Newgrange (*Brugh na Bóinne*, the Fort of the Boyne) is excavated and open to the public. It is an outstanding national monument, consisting of a round mound of earth over a passage leading into a

burial chamber. The passage is nineteen meters long, leading to a cruciform chamber about six meters by six meters, and almost six meters high. The mound itself is eleven meters high and eighty-five meters in diameter, and the roof supporting it is made of layers of stone lintels, narrowing inward to the top. But the crowning glory of this burial place of old is that on one day of the year, December 21 (the Winter Solstice), the sun shines through the roof-box over the door, along the passage, to illuminate the burial chamber.

50   *Scarecrow near Dingle, Co. Kerry.*

Inside the chamber, Newgrange, Co. Meath.

Is iomaí lá sa chill orainn.

We owe the grave many a day.

In a quiet water'd land, a land of roses,
Stands Saint Kieran's city fair;
And the warriors of Erin in their famous
   generations
Slumber there.

So begins T. W. Rolleston's translation of the fourteenth-century Irish poem, "The Dead at Clonmacnoise." Clonmacnoise is no ordinary graveyard. It is the site of one of Ireland's foremost early monasteries, and it lies on the east bank of the Shannon River in County Offaly, nine miles, by boat, from Athlone. It was founded by Saint Ciarán who came downriver from County Roscommon in 545 A.D. The remains (comprising eight churches, two round towers, three high crosses, over four hundred early gravestones, and two holy wells) are of exceptional interest to the student of early Irish art and architecture.

Clonmacnoise was ravaged by fire thirteen times between 722 and 1205. It was plundered by the Vikings eight times between 832 and 1163, and Irish enemies assailed it no less than twenty-seven times in the same period. English foes plundered it six times between 1178 and 1204, and it was finally reduced to complete ruin by the English garrison of Athlone in 1552, when "not a bell, large or small, or an image, or an altar, or a book, or a gem, or even glass in a window, was left which was not carried away" (Killanin and Duignan, 1967). Later in "The Dead at Clonmacnoise" we read:

Many and many a son of Conn, the Hundred-Fighter,
In the red earth lies at rest;

Many a blue eye of Clan Colman the turf covers,
Many a swan-white breast.

Aerial view of Clonmacnoise, Co. Offaly.

53

Ní túisce craiceann na seanchaorach ar an bhfraigh ná craiceann na caorach óige.

The skin of the old sheep is on the rafter no sooner than the skin of the young sheep.

"The younger person has no guarantee of outliving the older."

The sheep has a well-earned place in Irish proverbs because rural Irish people for centuries depended on sheep for their clothing. Most people kept their own sheep and, using the traditional skills that were handed down to them from earlier generations, transformed the wool off the sheep's back into warm clothing for themselves and their families.

The first step was to cut the fleece off the sheep with a scissors-like implement called "shears." The wool was then picked clean of pieces of heather or furze that might be caught in it, before being sprinkled with oil to make it easier to tease and to card. The teasing or carding was done with a pair of special wire brushes called "cards." A small amount of wool was placed on one of these, and it was combed or teased by pulling the two cards against one another. A small amount of wool was left in a little roll, ready for spinning, and the rest of the fleece was prepared in the same manner.

One of these rolls was then attached to the spindle of the spinning wheel and, by turning the wheel, was spun into a thread. Another roll and then another was attached to the previous one, and soon all the fleece was transformed into a single thread, or "weft" (*inneach*). This thread could be doubled and spun again to make it stronger, and this stronger thread was called "warp" (*dlúth*). The weaver would later weave together these threads to make the cloth or frieze, using the weft threads as the crosswise threads of the fabric and the warp threads as the lengthwise threads of the fabric. Before bringing the two threads to the weaver, however, the warp had to be put on a warp-frame, to have it ready for the weaver's frame. The weft did not need any framing.

Sheep at Aasleagh Falls, Co. Mayo.

Carding wool.

Maireann an chraobh ar an bhfál ach ní mhaireann an lámh do chuir.

The branch lives on the hedge but the hand that planted it is dead.

A very common and thought-provoking experience in rural Ireland, especially in the west of Ireland, is to come upon the ruins of an old house, lying forsakenly on the side of a mountain or in a lonely valley, without another house, old or new, anywhere to be seen. Such a scene is likely to evoke unhappy memories of emigration, especially the emigration that followed the Great Famine of 1845–1848.

The rate of emigration increased during the years immediately before the Great Famine, and it greatly increased during and after the famine itself. There were, however, thousands of people who could not afford to emigrate, which prompted a charitable English Quaker, James Hack Tuke, to introduce what was to be known as "The Free Emigration Scheme" in the years 1882–1884. It is estimated that ten thousand people from the west of Ireland availed themselves of this scheme to emigrate to America.

In an effort to alleviate the poverty in congested districts in the west of Ireland, in 1891 the government founded the Congested Districts Board, which organized the building of roads and piers and instructed the people in new methods of fishing, farming, and various crafts. State-sponsored housing schemes helped to change the housing pattern in many of the poorer districts of rural Ireland, and houses built under these schemes are instantly recognizable because of their uniformity of plan and materials.

Emigration continued right through this century and reached a peak in the fifties, to ebb almost entirely in the seventies. For the past few years, however, the emigrant ship and now more often the jumbo jet to America is full to capacity again. So much so, in fact, that today thousands of young Irish are illegal aliens in the United States of America.

Glenties (na Gleannta), Co. Donegal.

Níl a fhios ag aon duine cá bhfuil fód a bháis.

Nobody knows where his sod of death is.

Graves and crosses at Caherciveen, Co. Kerry

Keel Strand, Achill, Co. Mayo.

59

Group of people in Casla, Connemara, Co. Galway.

Types of People
Cineálacha Daoine

Máirtín Ó Cadhain, who died in 1970, is regarded by many as one of the greatest Irish writers of the twentieth century. As a young man he made a collection of folktales for the Folklore Commission and in a public lecture on his own writing the year before he died, he spoke of the difficulty he experienced in resisting the temptation to use folklore in some of his creative work.

Happily, however, he did not resist the temptation to use a style that is very common in the many proverbs he grew up with in south Connemara. An example is his use of the adjective instead of the noun to describe a person or character. Thus he speaks of *an santach* (the greedy) instead of *an duine santach* (the greedy person). This was to become one of the hallmarks of Ó Cadhain's writing, and although he said himself that he first noticed it in the poetry of the seventeenth century, he also acknowledges a debt to the proverbs.

The public lecture mentioned above was published under the title *Páipéir Bhána agus Páipéir Bhreaca (White Papers and Speckled Papers)*. In it he describes the "local organic community" in which he grew up:

It had its virtues and its vices, *meitheal* and cooperation and neighbourly obligingness on the day of distress, but uproar and fighting and jealousy also. There was the loafer (*leadaí*) and the thief (*bradaí*), the man who would remember, if he found your donkey in his field, that there was a donkey in the stable when Christ was being born there. And there was the other fellow, even if the donkey said up to his mouth that it was on its own back, above all other donkeys of the world and of history, that Christ rode into Jerusalem, who would drive horseshoe nails through its back, in spite of that. (Translated from the Irish.)

In the following proverbs we meet the traveler and the roamer (*siúlach*), the teller of tales and the gossiper (*scéalach*), the full and plenty (*sách*), the lean and hungry (*seang*), the card-playing gambler (*cearbhach*), and many others.

Máirtín Ó Cadhain (1906–1970).

Old time threshing, Co. Kerry.

61

Bíonn siúlach scéalach.

The traveler has tales to tell.

"The roamer is a gossiper."

There is a long tradition in Ireland of wandering scholars, clerics, poets, musicians, tailors, stonemasons, tinsmiths, and laborers. These people helped to keep the oral tradition alive, and the wandering laborer (*spailpín*) was very often a poet and storyteller as well. Many houses had a special bed or straw mat for those fairly regular visitors who were always welcome for their songs and stories and because of the news they carried from distant parts.

Traveling people were formerly known as "tinkers" as they were, until recently, mainly tinsmiths, who mended pots and pans and broken crockery in country houses before the "plastic revolution" put an end to their ancient trade. Thousands of them are still on the road, but many have been integrated into the settled community as a result of a resettlement program by a group of voluntary lay people. Some of the men still carry on the tradition of bartering horses, while the women sell small articles or beg from door to door.

Seán Ó Súilleabháin, the folklorist, reminds us that descendants of Irish travelers who emigrated to the United States more than a hundred years ago still carry on their nomadic life there. They may number ten thousand or so and range from the coast of Georgia to as far west as Oklahoma (*Encyclopaedia of Ireland*, "People of the Roads").

Peddlers of various kinds, selling pins, laces, thread, tobacco, tea, and other goods, have traveled along the Irish roads for centuries but are now rarely seen. (In recent years their place has been taken by peddlers from the Indian Punjab and Pakistan.) There were also travelers who bought and collected eggs and hand-knitted stockings, and, more recently, old clothes, rags, and feathers, but almost all have disappeared from the Irish scene.

Travelers, Dunboyne, Co. Meath.

Súil le cúiteamh a mhilleas an cearrbhach.

Hope to recoup is what ruins the card player (gambler).

John Dunton, an Englishman who traveled in Ireland at the end of the seventeenth century, mentions the Irish country people's love for the "game of five cards." It is more than likely that the games he saw being played nearly three hundred years ago were the same games we play today. Card playing in rural Ireland barely survived the arrival of television in the early sixties, but in recent years it has again become popular.

The games of "fifteen," "twenty-five," "forty-five," "a hundred and ten," and others, are gaining back their former popularity in parts of rural Ireland. For the beginner the precedence of the cards may seem very complicated. The five of trumps (the turned up suit) has the highest value, followed by the jack of trumps, the ace of hearts, the ace of trumps, the king of trumps, and the queen of trumps. Discounting face cards, all red cards increase in value as they go up in number, and all black cards decrease in value as they go up in number. The eight of hearts or diamonds, for example, will beat the seven of hearts or diamonds, whereas the seven of spades or clubs will beat the eight of spades or clubs.

It is not known who invented playing cards or where they came from, but card playing was solidly established in Europe by the end of the fourteenth century and in Ireland by the sixteenth century. There are accounts of card players who publicly gambled away all their clothing and dressed themselves in straw or leaves, and many laws prohibiting card playing were introduced in the sixteenth and seventeenth centuries.

There were many ways of bringing luck in playing cards. A needle stuck in a player's clothing, or a woman sewing or knitting sitting behind him, could bring luck. Money received from the sale of eggs was lucky, and a card player often exchanged coins with his wife or mother, since the egg money always belonged to the housewife. Bad luck could be reversed by turning one's cap back to front or turning one's coat inside out. Persistent bad luck might be caused by sitting directly under a rafter, but some cynics maintain that the dislike of sitting under a rafter came from the old days when the hens were kept in the house and perched on the rafters (Kevin Danaher, *In Ireland Long Ago*).

Card players.

Playing cards in Terry's (McDonagh's) Bar, Rossaveal, Connemara, Co. Galway.

Ní thuigeann an sách an seang.

The well-fed does not understand the lean.

"Let them eat cake," the remark attributed to Marie Antoinette, Queen of France, when she was told that the rioting poor of Paris had no bread at the time of the French Revolution, is the expression that is often quoted to illustrate the lack of understanding by the rich of the poor.

The person who has never experienced poverty or hunger will have difficulty understanding the plight of the poor and the needy. The poor will always have a better chance of getting alms from those who are only slightly better off than themselves, and many beggars have learned to steer clear of the houses of the very rich.

Class distinction in sport, as in all other aspects of life, is still manifest in Ireland although it is fast disappearing. Foxhunting on horseback is still the preserve of the better-off while the less well-off have their own types of hunting. One of these involves sending ferrets into rabbit burrows to kill and retrieve the rabbits or to chase them out into the open where the lean greyhound can give chase.

This difference between the hunting habits of the rich and poor, like most other differences in Ireland, is not without its humor. There is a story told about a well-to-do hunting man standing with other churchgoers outside a church after Mass on a fine Sunday morning. He shouts across to a colleague, "Are you going hunting today, George?" to which the colleague replies, "No, Arthur, the mare has sprained a fetlock." On hearing this exchange, a not so well-off wag in the crowd shouts across to a colleague of his own, "Are you going hunting today, Dinny?" to which Dinny replies, "No, Timmy, the ferret has the flu."

Galway Blazers Hunt.

Is teann gach madra gearr i ndoras a thí féin.

Every short dog (terrier) is bold in the doorway of its own house.

This proverb goes back to a time when country people had to travel long distances on foot and had occasion to pass many a bold dog on many a doorstep. There were houses where they knew they were welcome and houses they learned to avoid, and it is often said that the dog on the doorstep is as friendly or as hostile as the people inside.

The house in the photograph is a typical subsistence farming unit common in south Connemara in the first half of this century. The household grew its own potatoes and vegetables. The family kept its own cow or two, sheep, a horse or donkey, and maybe a pig. They saved their own turf (peat), hay, and oats, and kept hens, geese, or ducks. If they lived near the sea they probably had a currach for fishing and perhaps a wooden boat for bringing ashore seaweed for fertilizer from the little seaweed-covered rock islands in the bay.

Cash income was minimal and consisted of an old-age pension, children's allowances, and (after 1933) the social welfare assistance known as the "dole." This might be supplemented by selling a few truckloads of turf to be shipped to the Aran Islands. Centuries of turf-cutting for the home fires and for commercial gain has stripped most of south Connemara to the bare rock. The man of the house might own a turf-boat (Galway Hooker), as they were very plentiful along the Connemara coast until the middle of this century. If not, he probably did seasonal work in England or Scotland or worked for a farmer in East Galway.

A large family lived in every house and if a child did well enough at primary school to earn a scholarship, there was the possibility of a job as a teacher or civil servant. Without such a scholarship, however, the future often held nothing better than the emigrant ship to England, or preferably to America.

It was of these people that Máirtín Ó Cadhain wrote, in his short story "The Year 1912," that they were a race "whose guardian angel was the American trunk, whose guiding star was the exile ship, whose Red Sea was the Atlantic."

Homestead in Lettermullen, Connemara, Co. Galway.

69

Is í an dias is troime is ísle a chromas a ceann.

It is the heaviest ear of grain that bends its head the lowest.

Here we have the unmistakable message that substance should always be accompanied by humility. Although the proverb usually refers to a person's ability to carry learning lightly, it is also quoted when a rich or powerful person is seen to be humble as well.

There is an expression in Irish with which you greet a person you are delighted to see: "Seeing you is like seeing the new (season's) barley" (*Is í an eorna nua tú a fheiceáil*). This is a reminder of a time, in the west of Ireland, when homegrown barley bread was a welcome change from potatoes and Indian meal. People grew their own barley or rye, threshed the grain, winnowed it with a winnowing tray or sieve, ground it in a quern,

Harvest scene.

and baked the whole-meal bread on the open hearth.

The flail, with which most people threshed the grain, consisted of two sticks loosely tied together at the ends. One of the sticks was held in the hands while the grain was beaten with the other. Some people threshed their grain by lashing it on a stone, and still others burned it from the straw. The burning method had the added advantage of drying the grain, whereas the lashing method left straw that was ideal for thatching. The threshing machine took over from the flails in mainland Europe in the nineteenth century, but it was not used in some parts of the west of Ireland until well into the twentieth century.

Flour was a delicacy to be afforded by the poor at Christmas only, when people brought their oats to the mill to be ground. In Connemara in the last century, the week before Christmas was the miller's busiest week of the year. Even though watermills were plentiful, people often had to line up, and it is reported that a plug of tobacco was the best bribe to give the miller if you wanted to get away early. The miller's official reward was every fifth quart of the grain.

The ancient but illicit art of distilling poteen (*poitín*) from barley is still being practiced. Poteen is often referred to as "the juice of the barley" (*sú na heorna*).

Threshing grain.

70

Stooks of oats, Carraroe, Co. Galway.

Paddy Glackin, fiddle; Joe Heaney; Mairéad Ní Dhomhnaill,
traditional Irish singer; Tony McMahon, accordion; and Liam
Óg Ó Floinn, pipes, at a folk concert at the National Concert
Hall in Dublin in September, 1982.

Is buaine clú ná saol.

Fame is more lasting than life.

Seosamh Ó hÉanaí (Joe Heaney), the renowned *sean-nós* (old-style or traditional) Irish singer from Carna in Connemara was the first non-American to be awarded an American National Heritage Award by the National Endowment for the Arts, at a special ceremony during the annual Folklife Festival in Washington, D.C. in July 1982. "In honoring Joe Heaney, we are celebrating the quality of his art and paying tribute to the enormous contribution he has made to the fabric of American life," said Arts Endowment Chairman Frank Hodsoll at the ceremony.

When Joe Heaney sang publicly in Dublin for the first time, the Irish language writer Máirtín Ó Cadhain wrote of him:

In *Caoineadh na dTrí Muire (The Lament of the Three Marys)* he brings home to us the joys and sorrows of Mary with the intimacy and poignancy of a Fra Angelico painting. This *tour de force* forms between him and his audience a bond of sympathy which has scarcely been felt between any audience and actor in this city in our time.

Joe Heaney inherited the art of *sean-nós* singing—an unaccompanied and highly ornamented style of traditional singing—from his parents and grandparents and the generations before them. The Irish-speaking district of Carna, where he was born in 1919 and buried in 1984, is famous for its wealth of songs and folklore. He spent most of his

Joe Heaney.

early adult life in Scotland and England, and though his consummate artistry was appreciated by a small group of people, it was not until he settled in the United States in the mid-sixties that he was given the recognition he deserved.

He became well known at folk festivals and concerts held in various parts of the U.S., and in 1976 he was invited to join the Folklore Department at Wesley University in Connecticut. A course in Irish Culture

was offered there under the direction of Professor Neilly Bruce. In 1982 he transferred to the University of Washington, Seattle, at the invitation of Dr. Fred Leibermann, head of the Ethnomusicology Division. There he served as a visiting artist and lectured on *sean-nós* singing, storytelling, and other aspects of Irish culture and folk tradition.

Following his death in Seattle in May 1984, the Joe Heaney Memorial Fund was established there. This fund, together with continued support from the National Endowment for the Arts, has enabled the university's archives to develop the Joe Heaney Collection. The collection consists of non-commercial recordings of approximately 250 songs and 100 stories and anecdotes, in both Irish and English.

Poet Michael Davitt, a good friend of Joe Heaney's, wrote a poem entitled "Poem for Joe":

Your arrival was a breath of old times
Symbols of your native sod that you
had brought with you abroad, were
back with you again over threshold:
The shoe lace that tied your road-weary
suitcase and that vulgar laugh, the
laugh of a man out of whom the years
hadn't sifted the boy and whose foyer
manners hadn't got the better of his
fireside manners—you were to show
us again later on that your stage

manners were without blemish.

We lived for a month in the sean-nós.
Your turf-voice transcending the semi-
detached suburban greyness—your
sad open-hearthed eyes, your yarns
about the old life in Carna, your daily
excursions in search of fresh mackerel around the street markets of
Dublin, your curses on the tea-powder
in the bags no matter how black we
made it—you needed strong evidence
of leaves at the bottom of every mug.
You put rhyme and rigmarole in the
mouths of the children and you even
made the potatoes sing, pushing
their stomachs out in celebration.

When you closed your eyes at night, we
would walk with you down the back-
roads, barefoot, lilting, gathering aislingí
on Trá Bháin.

(*aislingí* dreams, *Trá Bháin* White Strand)

Dublin street art, Bloomsday, 1984.

74

An té thabharfas scéal chugat tabharfaidh sé dhá scéal uait.

He who comes with a story to you will bring two away from you.

Men walking their dogs, St. Stephen's Green, Dublin.

Ní scéal rúin é ó tá a fhios ag triúr é.

It is not a secret if it is known to three people.

Bus stop, Galway.

Gloucester Street, Dublin.

Is iad na muca ciúinc a ithcas an mhin.

It is the quiet pigs that eat the meal.

"Quiet people are well able to look after themselves."

Long before George Orwell's English pig, Major, headed the dictatorship in *Animal Farm*, the Irish pig had its place in literature well established. In the Fenian tale, *The Pursuit of Diarmaid and Gráinne (Tóraíocht Dhiarmada agus Ghráinne)*, it was a magic pig that killed the hero Diarmaid, on top of Ben Bulben, in what is now called Yeats Country in Co. Sligo. In the witty and satirical twelfth century text, *The Vision of Mac Conglinne (Aisling Mhic Conglinne)*, many references are made to the various types of pig meat, and pig meat still has a place of honor on the Irish breakfast table.

After the Earls of Tyrone and Tyrconnell, O'Neill and O'Donnell, fled to Europe in 1607, a series of poems in Irish appeared bewailing the downfall of the great Irish families. In one of these poems, Séathrún Céitinn (Geoffrey Keating), a Co. Tipperary priest and scholar, uses the Biblical image of the cockle growing through pure Irish seed. He addresses Ireland and says, "Not a drop is left in the plain of your pure white breast—drained dry by the litter of every alien sow."

James Joyce, three hundred years later, referred to Ireland itself as "the old sow that eats her own farrow." Modern Irish writers are still fascinated by the pig and at least two of our living poets have devoted a poem to the ritual, in rural Ireland, of killing the pig.

Pork in its various forms has always been popular in Ireland, but there are parts of Scotland where it was never eaten. This taboo was attributed to the Pictish origins of the people in the Eastern and Central Highlands, as the Gaelic and Norse settlers in Scotland had no such aversion to the pig.

In Ireland today the rivers are under a massive pollution threat from pig slurry produced by intensive pig-fattening farms. All too often some of this lethal pollutant is released into the rivers and the "quiet pigs" who are responsible should be brought to heel.

Sow and litter.

An té a bhfuil bólacht ar cnoc aige ní bhíonn suaimhneas ar sop aige.

He who has cattle on the hill will not sleep easy.

Tory Island, Co. Donegal.

Friends and Neighbors
Cairde agus Comharsana

In rural Ireland, as in all small farming communities, a contradiction has always existed between the importance placed on having good neighbors and the desire of each household to be self-sufficient and independent. This is reflected in the many contradictory proverbs we have in Irish about neighbors and neighborliness.

Reliance on the extended family, which had the sanction of our ancient laws, still lingers on in some rural communities. Neighborliness was often based on kinship, as many of one's neighbors were also relatives. Although a household could almost always rely on a small circle of relatives without any sense of obligation, there were many occasions when the help and reliability of a near neighbor was invaluable.

When a needy housewife's only source of income was the sale of fresh eggs to the local shopkeeper, she could always borrow a few eggs to make up the score or half score and pay back the eggs when her own hens laid. If she ran out of flour and did not have enough money put together to buy a bag, she could borrow some from the neighbor and give it back later. In my own native Connemara the measure for borrowed flour was a small tin can that held a quart, whereas the measure for borrowed sugar was a cup, and for borrowed tea an eggstand (egg cup). As these commodities had to be bought in the shop, they were scrupulously paid back, but other borrowed necessities like milk or turf were not expected to be returned. The borrowed pinch of salt, however, was always paid back, as it was considered unlucky not to do so.

Bitterness and hostility existed among neighbors at times, often caused by someone striking a neighbor's thieving dog or cow, and often ending up in a court of law, as the following proverbs suggest.

81

Má bhuaileann tú mo mhadra buailfidh tú mé féin.

If you hit my dog you hit myself.

The partnership of man and dog is a very ancient one, especially in farming communities. A seventh-century text stated that "he who kills a dog that guards the flocks or stays in the house shall pay five cows for the dog and supply a dog of the same breed and restore whatever wild animals eat from the flock until the end of the year." The clever little sheepdog that can almost read its master's mind by day and can guard the household by night has a very special place in the

farmer's home. An assault by an outsider on this special animal is taken by the members of the household as an assault on themselves. Even pet dogs in urban communities can cause neighbor to be set against neighbor.

There is a tradition in the west of Ireland, when admiring an animal, always to say "God bless it." There was a superstition that if you did not utter that blessing, you could cast what was known as the "evil eye" on the animal. There were two animals, however—the dog and the cat—considered unworthy of God's blessing, and young children were warned never to say "God bless it" to either of the two, as they were supposed to be connected with the Devil.

According to legend, the first dog and cat were the son and daughter of an unlikely marriage between an Irish farmer and the Devil's mother, who appeared to the farmer as a beautiful woman and asked him to marry her. It was around the time Saint Patrick came to Ireland and it was the saint who noticed the evil appearance of the woman and told the farmer that she was the Devil's mother. With the husband's consent, Saint Patrick banished her from the house in a ball of flame, and then he decided to leave the two children to be of service to the people. He changed the daughter into a cat and the son into a dog, and that is why, according to the legend, there has been something human about the dog and the cat ever since.

Poulnabrone Dolmen and dog, Co. Clare.

Salcarragh, Co. Donegal.

Casla, Connemara, Co. Galway.

Déan an fál nó íocfaidh tú foghail.

Make the fence or you will pay for the plunder.

Stone fields, Connemara, Co. Galway.

Is maith an scáthán súil charad.

A friend's eye is a good mirror.

Mother and son, Connemara, Co. Galway.

Is maith an capall a tharraingíos a charr féin.

It is a good horse that draws its own cart.

The image of the blinkered, hard-working draft horse, clearly minding its own business, contrasts starkly with that of the inquisitive neighbor who pokes his nose into everybody's affairs. The teaming of man and horse, whether in the streets of big cities or on remote farms, is a very old tradition that has now almost come to an end in Ireland. The cart horse was made redundant by the truck and the plough horse by the tractor, and the ancient trades of the blacksmith and the harness-maker have almost disappeared. Very few farmers follow the plough nowadays and the unnecessary farm horses were shipped to the continent of Europe in the 1950s to be fed as horsemeat to our European neighbors.

Horseflesh is still not eaten in Ireland, perhaps because the horse was once regarded as a sacred animal, or perhaps because early churchmen believed that horses were associated with pagan rites. The skulls of horses and cows have been found under the floors of homes in many parts of Ireland. It is thought that this custom replaced an earlier custom of burying live animals in the foundations of houses in order to placate the spirits. Moreover, the sacrifice of live horses and cows almost certainly replaced an earlier pagan rite of human sacrifice, and, according to legend, Saint Columcille's brother Dobhrán was buried alive to placate the spirits before a church could be built on the Scottish island of Iona in 563 A.D.

Even in recent times, in many parts of Ireland the horse was believed to be sensitive to the presence of evil spirits, and horses have often taken fright at seeing or perceiving something not visible to the human eye. There are stories in our folklore of water horses living in rivers and lakes that would often come ashore at night to mate with local mares. Many of the draft mares now left in the country are used specifically for mating with the modern-day version of the water horse, the thoroughbred sire. Their offspring, the famous Irish racehorses, hunters, and show jumpers, are now famous all over the world.

Dublin scene.

Is fearr glas ná amhras.

A lock is better than suspicion.

Peig Sayers (1873–1958), the Blasket Island author, was noted for her storytelling and for her seemingly inexhaustible store of proverbs. While in domestic service with a particularly mean farming couple outside Dingle, Peig tells of having to watch the farmer and his wife tuck into roast mutton, sweet bread, and tea (which was very scarce at the time), while she herself went hungry. When the couple had finished eating, the woman of the house put the roast meat and all the rest of the food away in the cupboard under lock and key and they both went out for the day, as it was a holy day.

One of Peig's many proverbs, "Necessity knows no law" (*Níl aon dlí ar an riachtanas*), may well have inspired her to get at the food. The cupboard had two doors, one of them under lock and key, and the other secured by two latches on the inside. By prizing a thin knife between the door and the frame, Peig managed to lift the two latches and open one of the doors. Her problem now was that the roast mutton was firmly embedded in the thick grease of the roasting pan, so that if she touched it at all it would be noticed. Undeterred, Peig placed the roasting pan over the fire until the grease melted and, to make a long story short, she ate her fill and treated herself to a nice cup of tea. Another problem now presented itself, and that was how to close the door again. By tying a piece of thread to each of the latches, she kept them lifted while clos-

The cupboard.

ing the door, and by pulling the threads the latches fell into place. Once everything was locked up in the cupboard again, she felt a new woman.

Several hours later, when the woman of the house returned, she had some new potatoes with her and suggested to Peig, rather sardonically, that she must be starving. Peig's response was to quote a well-known proverb:

"The well-fed is not perceptive of the hungry" (*Ní mhothaíonn an sách an t-ocrach*) said I to her. She did not notice anything and she did not expect that I could take anything out of the cupboard as she had locked it tight. She figured out that it was no use having suspicion, because the proverb says that "a lock is better than suspicion."

88

The thorn.

Is beag an dealg a dhéanas sileadh.

Even a small thorn causes festering.

Just as a small thorn, if not immediately removed, can cause pain and festering, so can the thoughtless word cause pain and hurt, and can very often be the cause of hostility among neighbors. (Some of the menfolk of former generations tended to give the proverb a more literal meaning and used it as a warning to their daughters to be careful when keeping company with men.)

Thorns have always been an occupational hazard for the farming community, but they were even more so when furze bushes played a very important role in day-to-day life in rural Ireland. A nineteenth-century farming manual describes the furze-cutting laborer who "saves himself from the prickles by an encasement of rough, untanned leather upon his left leg, which in the operation of faggoting he presses firmly on the branch to be cut down, while with his left hand, similarly guarded to the elbow, he holds the portion that he is about to cut down with his uplifted right hand."

Kevin Danaher has documented the many and varied uses the furze bush was put to in the past (*In Ireland Long Ago*). Laborers were constantly employed to cut it down with a billhook into stumps about a foot long. It was then packed into bundles and sold in the marketplaces in the cities and towns. The stack of furze was as common a sight as the stack of turf. Furze was prized as a fuel for the baking of bread on the open hearth with the griddle or the pot-oven, or in the brick ovens used by the town bakers and in some of the larger houses. Another important use of furze was as a foodstuff for the livestock, who were fed fresh, young, green shoots that had been chopped and crushed.

Castar na daoine ar a chéile ach ní chastar na cnoic ná na sléibhte.

People meet one another but the hills and the mountains don't.

"People meet but mountains never greet."

Meeting on bicycles, Co. Laois.

Bicycling on Achill Island, Co. Mayo.

Giorraíonn beirt bóthar.

Two shorten the road.

I ngan fhios don dlí is fearr bheith ann.

It is better to exist unknown to the law.

John Millington Synge's famous play, *The Playboy of the Western World*, is based on a story the playwright heard on one of his many visits to Inishmaan (*Inis Meáin*, Middle Island), in the Aran Islands in Galway Bay. The story is about a Connacht man who killed his father with the blow of a spade and then fled to Inishmaan, where the people hid him from the law and shipped him safely to America. In his book, *The Aran Islands*, Synge (1871–1909) has the following to say about law and justice:

This impulse to protect the criminal is universal in the west. It seems partly due to the association between justice and the hated English jurisdiction, but more directly to the primitive feeling of these people, who are never criminals yet always capable of crime, that a man will not do wrong unless he is under the influence of a passion which is as irresponsible as a storm on the sea. If a man has killed his father, and is already sick and broken with remorse, they can see no reason why he should be dragged away and killed by the law.

The most intelligent man on Inishmaan has often spoken to me of his contempt for the law, and of the increase of crime the police have brought to Aranmór. On this island, he says, if men have a little difference, or a little fight, their friends take care it does not go too far, and in a little time it is forgotten. In Kilronan there is a band of men paid to make out cases for themselves; the moment a blow is struck they come down and arrest the man who gave it. The other man he quarrelled with has to give evidence against him; whole families come down to the court and swear against each other till they become bitter enemies.

Security, Dublin.

95

Discussing life in Galway City.

Is beo duine gan a chairdre ach ní beo duine gan a phíopa.

One may live without one's friends but not without one's pipe.

The Liberties, Dublin

Inishmaan, Aran Islands.

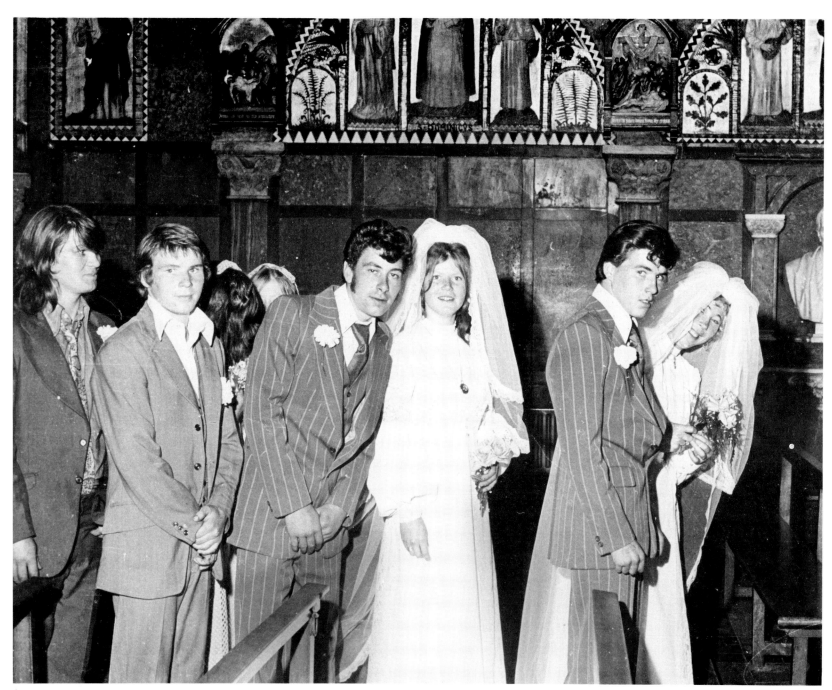

Double wedding, Dublin.

Women and Marriage
Mná agus Pósadh

So many of our Irish proverbs portray women in such unflattering and disparaging terms that it is difficult to give any credence to the suggestion that a nation's proverbs are a reflection of the popular character. Typical examples are: "Three things without rule, a woman, a pig and a mule." (*Trí ní gan riail, bean, muc agus múille*); "A pig is bolder than a goat but a woman surpassed the Devil" (*Is dána muc ná gabhar ach sháraigh bean an diabhal*); "Every expensive thing, the wish of every woman" (*Gach ní daor, mian gach mná*).

Love songs in Irish, on the other hand, are so full of exalted sentiments in describing a man's love for a woman, that one is inclined to be astonished at the contrast. There are, of course, proverbs in Irish in praise of women, but they are few in number: "Woe to him who does not follow a good woman's advice" (*Mairg nach ndéanann comhairle deámhná*), "A good housewife is half a life" (*Is leath beatha bean mhaith tí*), "Empty and cold is a house without a woman" (*Is folamh, fuar teach gan bean*).

Marriage is also treated with cynicism in Irish proverbs: "A man without wife or family is a man who has little fear of anybody" (*Fear gan bhean gan chlann, fear gan bheann ar aon duine*), "The gold disappears but the foolish woman remains" (*Imíonn an t-ór ach fanann an óinseach*), "There is no torture without marriage and no feast without roasting" (*Ní céasta go pósta agus ní féasta go róstadh*) set the general mood.

Bíonn a dteanga ina bpóca ag na mná go bpósann siad.

Women keep their tongue in their pocket until they marry.

The inference here is that women wait until they have the security of marriage before they begin to assert themselves. In the case of matchmade marriages, which were very common in rural Ireland until recently, they had very little choice. Very often a woman met her husband-to-be for the first time when he visited her house in the company of a matchmaker to ask her parents for her hand in marriage. It was customary to bring a bottle of whiskey along. It was a sign of the purpose of the visit and the whiskey made it easier for all concerned to discuss business. The young woman herself usually remained silent.

If the matchmaker convinced the girl's parents that the man with the bottle was a suitable match for their daughter, they then discussed a dowry, which consisted of cows or cash (or a combination of both). The girl's parents would sometimes visit the man's house and holding to see if it was a suitable place for their daughter to settle into. More often than not, if the parents agreed to the match, the daughter consented to the marriage and a wedding date was arranged. There was music and dancing in the bride's house the night before the marriage and in the groom's house the following day and night. The nearest thing to a honeymoon was the "month's visit" (*cuairt mhíosa*), a visit of the bride to her parents' home a month after the wedding. Tradition forbade her to visit her old home before that, the idea being that at least a month was needed to sever her connections with her parents and to get used to her new man and her new house. "Running home to her parents" would be interpreted by the neighbors as a sign that the marriage was not successful, and that impression had to be avoided at all cost.

Women with shawls, Carraroe, Co. Galway.

Going home after confirmation, Carraroe, Co. Galway.

Ón lá a bpósfaidh tú beidh do chroí i do bhéal agus do lámh i do phóca.

From the day you marry your heart will be in your mouth and your hand in your pocket.

There is a striking contrast between the cynicism of this proverb and the sentiment expressed in the following verses from the popular Irish love song *Glen Nephin* (*Cuaichín Ghleann Néifinn*). The verse translation is by Brian O'Rourke and it is found in his book of Gaelic folk songs with English translations, *Blas Meala* (*A Sip from the Honey Pot*):

My love lives in a distant valley, and it's the
    sweetest of all places,
Every treetop bends down with berries and
    every blossom spreads round its fragrance.
Oh, if my darling and I were married and our
    good fortune did not fail us,
The golden sovereigns in our pockets would
    pay the lady of the alehouse.

But the sunshine is drowned in darkness, the
    light of stars and moon is waning,
And the pathways I cannot master, for my own
    eyesight is surely fading,
With bitter tears for that sweet lady whose kiss
    of honey I've never tasted;
And, O my darling, relieve my hardship, for
    it's your charms that have me wasted.

So I will quit now this bitter townland, for it
    has left me sick and broken,
And I'll go seeking my only sweetheart in every
    place where her name is spoken.
Oh, the teardrops they have me blinded, the
    clearest signpost I cannot follow,
And it's my heartache I will not wake where
    you lay your dark hair on your pillow.

Is é do mhac do mhac go bpósann sé ach is í d'iníon d'iníon go bhfaighidh tú bás.

Your son is your son until he marries but your daughter is your daughter until you die.

Dublin wedding (with groom missing).

Ní ólann na mná leann ach imíonn sé lena linn.

Women do not drink liquor but it disappears when they are present.

Women with shawls, Coal Quay, Cork.

Is gaire do bhean leithscéal ná a naprún.

An excuse is nearer to a woman than her apron.

There are many stories found in Ireland which attempt to explain the origin of some human characteristics. The following is an attempt to explain "How Women Got an Excuse" and can be found in Seán Ó Sullivan's *Legends from Ireland:*

When our Saviour and His mother were travelling about long ago, He was starting to perform miracles at that time. They were walking along the road and met a blind man who was sitting at the side of it. When they passed by him the Virgin Mother remarked that the man was blind. "He is," said our Saviour, "And even so, there is his wife in that wood over there along with another man. I'm going to give the blind man his sight so that he can see her." "If you do," said His mother, "give the woman an excuse." No sooner did He say the word than the blind man rose to his feet and looked around in all directions. He looked towards the wood and saw his wife. She knew that he had seen her and she came towards him. When she came near, "You were in the wood with that man," said he. "If I hadn't been there, you wouldn't have got back your sight," said the wife. And that's how all women have got an excuse from that day to this.

Nuair is crua don chailleach caithfidh sí rith.

When the old woman is hard pressed she will have to run.

Cork woman with shawl.

Níl aon leigheas ar an ngrá ach pósadh.

The only cure for love is marriage.

The idea of love being a disease is often expressed with cynicism in Irish proverbs but with extreme romantic sentiment in many of the Irish love songs. The following verses are taken from a fairly typical man's love song called *The Little Field of Barley (An Goirtín Eornan)* translated from the Irish by Brian O'Rourke and found in his book, *Blas Meala (A Sip from the Honey Pot)*:

I am watching you, O little thrush, as in a bush
  you rest from flight;
If I trust you with my story, will you be sorry
  for my plight?
Take a secret letter to that girl with the golden
  curls and the eyes so bright,
That for love of her my heart will break and I
  lie awake all through the night.

The sky above has turned to mud, there's a
  roaring flood in the River Lee,
The snow has covered all the roads and the
  foam is frozen upon the sea;
The seals upon the rocks lie numb, and the
  birds fly dumb from tree to tree,
Since my sweetheart stole away the sun; she's
  the only one who could comfort me.

'Tis not your little field of barley, my darling, I
  am keen to gain,
And it's not the thought of all your wealth that
  has robbed my health and makes me
  complain;
It's not the want of herds has my heart parched,
  like the grass that's scorched for want of
  rain,
But the taste of your kiss upon my mouth could
  relieve my drought and ease my pain.

Stephen's Green, Dublin.

Is uaigneach an níochán nach mbíonn léine ann.

It is a lonely washing that has no (man's) shirt in it.

A very popular song in Irish is a woman's love song called *Castle O'Neill (Caisleán Uí Néill)*. The following verses are translated by Brian O'Rourke in *Blas Meala*:

Oh, farewell to last night; what delight if again
    I could be
With the handsome young rogue who would
    coax me awhile on his knee;
But since you betrayed me, I'm afraid I'll pay
    dear for my spree,
And a curse I call down on the mountains
    between you and me.

Oh, in Castle O'Neill is the thief who has stolen
    my bloom;
He could make the birds sleep in the trees with
    his sweetly played tune;
His laughing white teeth and his gleaming eye
    shine in the gloom,
Like a cool mountain stream sparkling clear in
    the bright sun at noon.

Oh, on the street outside an alehouse, I would
    make out the print of his heel,
On the bog I would know him as he loaded the
    turf in the creel;
If I owned all Tyrone, 'tis before him alone I
    would kneel,
In the hope that I could marry my darling in
    Castle O'Neill.

Oh, the taste of your kiss on my lips was the
    cause of my fall,
And with my grief for your leaving, my
    sweetheart, I can't sleep at all;
Oh, I've said many curses since the horses they
    broke down the wall,
And then plunged in the river and never
    returned to the stall.

Oh, there's no hill so high, love, that on it I
    would not know your walk;
There's no maiden so clever that she's never
    taken in by fine talk;
Now all my friends shun me, and I wonder
    where are all the kind folk,
And to see my child's father with another man's
    wife is no joke.

The washing hanging out to dry.

Más maith leat tú a cháineadh, pós.

If you want to be criticized, marry.

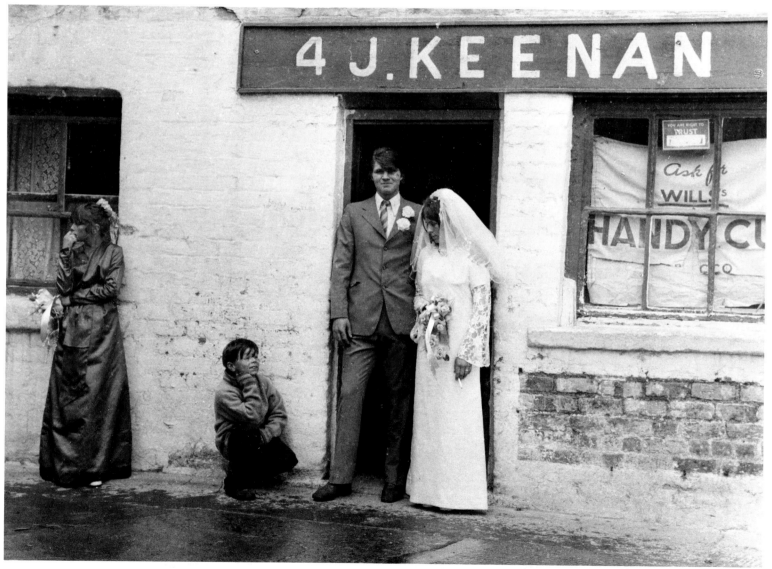

112

Wedding scene, Dublin.

An rud a líonas an tsúil líonann sé an croí.

What fills the eye fills the heart.

Winter scene, Stephen's Green, Dublin.

113

Bringing home the hay, Co. Dublin.

Work
Obair

Timothy O'Neill states in his book, *Life and Tradition in Rural Ireland:*

Man's principal activity in rural Ireland has always been agriculture and the various tasks associated with farming. Indeed it is only in the last decade that the balance in Irish society has changed, and now the majority of the population lives in urban areas. Up to the 1960s the Irish were mainly rural dwellers and even in the towns and villages the connections with the country were binding and strong. In the past the year's work for rural dwellers mainly involved securing their requirements for food, shelter and warmth. Most farmers attended their own crops, built their own houses, herded their own cattle, sheep and other animals and cut their own peat. The womenfolk were often equally engaged in these tasks, and added to them the making and repairing of clothes and cooking the family's food. Rural craftsmen were engaged in similar activities and the country weaver usually farmed his own plot of land. Even though a money economy has operated in most parts of Ireland for centuries, rural dwellers regarded self-sufficiency as normal and earnings were often only needed for the payment of rents, taxes and tithes. Many writers have remarked upon the Irishman's attachment to the land and when the history of the country is examined this is hardly surprising. The fortunes of families usually depended on the produce of the land, and only in the present century has the economy been diversified and the proportionate numbers engaged in agriculture decreased. In viewing life and tradition in rural Ireland the plough field and pasture are as important as the battlefield in charting the fortunes of ordinary countryfolk.

Is namhaid í an cheird gan í a fhoghlaim.

A trade not (properly) learned is an enemy.

This proverb is often quoted when a young or inexperienced person makes a mistake or causes an injury that a skilled or more experienced craftsman would have avoided. It is a negative form of the English proverb, "Practice makes perfect," and is also quoted when admiring a skilled person at work, whether wielding an adze in the ancient craft of boatbuilding or engraving a priceless piece of cut glass.

Waterford has been associated with cut glass since 1783, when it was the second most important port in Ireland. Waterford glass was famous in the eighteenth and nineteenth centuries but excessive export duties, together with lack of capital, caused the business to close down in 1851. Almost one hundred years later the industry was revived, and in 1951 Waterford Crystal began its second phase which was to take the company to the summit of the world's crystal industry.

Each crystal shape begins as a craftsman gathers a quantity of molten crystal from the furnace. This "gather" is collected on the end of a blowing iron with a twisting motion, and it is then smoothed with a wooden block and shaped to roughly correspond with the outline of the desired item. The craftsman then blows through the rod to create the cavity inside the crystal and, using a mold to control the outer shape, he blows the piece to its full size. Throughout the process his actions determine the wall thickness of the item being made, an essential factor in making Waterford crystal because of the great depth to which the various facets are cut later.

The molten crystal quickly sets to a solid form and is then "annealed"—a process that allows the crystal to reach normal air temperatures slowly, which is essential to avoid stresses caused by too rapid cooling and contraction. The implements used by the blower today are almost identical to those used by the glassmakers of the eighteenth and nineteenth centuries.

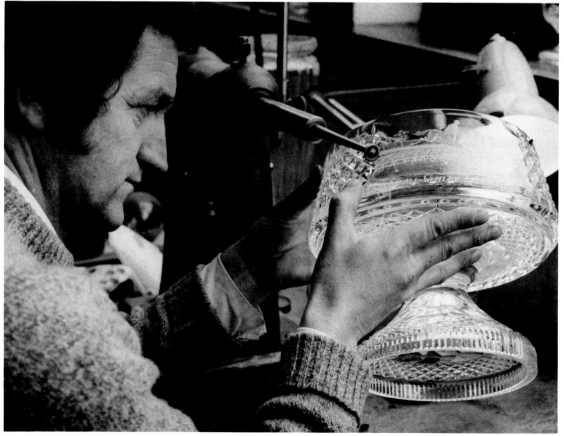

Waterford crystal being cut.

Boatwright with adze.

Dhá thrian den obair í an chosúlacht.

Two thirds of the work is the semblance.

The original version of the proverb was "Two thirds of the dance is the semblance" (*Dhá thrian den rince í an chosúlacht*). What is generally meant is that it is very important to "look the part" and to give the impression that you are doing whatever you are supposed to be doing, whether you are actually doing it or not.

Dodging work often occurred because of laziness, but it was sometimes a reaction to a hard taskmaster or because there was very little work to be done and the work had to be "spared." This was often true in the past when unemployed country laborers were given temporary work as road-maintenance men with the various county councils. It was in their interest to make the job last, as jobs were scarce, and groups of men were often seen along the roadside very busy at pretending to be working. The characteristic pose for such workers was leaning on their shovels, which was commonly known in Irish as *ag tabhairt cíoch don tsluasaid* (breast-feeding the shovel).

There is a story told of one of the first planeloads of American tourists approaching Shannon Airport in the late 1950s. One of the passengers looked down at the beautiful countryside and asked one of the Aer Lingus hostesses, "What are those black spots on the road down there?" to which she replied, "If they move they're crows, and if they don't they're county council workers."

Resting

Obair ó chrích obair bean tí.

Work without end is a housewife's work.

"A man's work is from sun to sun but a woman's work is never done."

Bringing home the turf, Gorumna Island, Connemara, Co. Galway.

Is olc an chearc nach scríobann di féin.

It is a bad hen that does not scratch for herself.

The hen is always seen as a busy provider and the message of the proverb is that we should all be able to provide for ourselves at least.

Hens were the most reliable source of food and money poor country people had in the old days, but they were often the cause of many an argument and many a bitter word between neighbors. This was often caused by a hen laying its eggs in a neighbor's field, or by a hen straying in among a neighbor's hens and choosing to remain there, possibly because the feeding was better.

In *An Old Woman's Reflections*, Peig Sayers gives a humorous account of just such a disagreement between two neighbors, Nora and Brigid, in Dunquin, Co. Kerry, at the beginning of this century:

"If I saw her I should recognize her," said Nora. Then Brigid stood up and put some food on a dish in the middle of the house and she called the hens. Soon there were over forty hens around the dish and a stranger of a big red cockerel with three inches of a big double comb on him, and he wouldn't prove a good share to anyone who would interfere with the hens.

"God with my soul! You have a flock of them!" said Nora.

"I have," said Brigid, "most of them stayed with me after my sister who went to America lately."

Nora was looking closely at them, and at last she stood up, and down with her to where they were eating. She caught the hen of the dissent and picked it up.

"That's the hen I gave to Maureen," said she. "Keep her or give her from you!"

Before the word was out of her mouth the cockerel had jumped out of himself and he was entangled in her legs and had a painful peck given to her in the back of her hand. She was anxious letting the hen go, because her legs were well scratched.

"Musha, it's an old proverb," said she, "and it's true, that the peacemaker doesn't go free!" (*Ní théann fear an réitigh as*), and she took herself out the door.

Feeding the hens, Casla, Connemara, Co. Galway.

An té a dtéann cáil na mochéirí amach dó ní miste dó codladh go méanlae.

He who gets a name for early rising can stay in bed until midday.

An old bed.

Roscommon Castle.

De réir a chéile a thógtar na caisleáin.

It takes time to build castles. "Rome was not built in a day."

Ní bheathaíonn na briathra na bráithre.

Mere words do not feed the friars.

The close similarity in Irish between its three key words lends special irony to this proverb, which may well have had its origins in the Middle Ages when mendicant friars, who were famous for their oratory, had to beg for their food. Nowadays it is quoted as a reminder that there has been enough talking and it is time to get some work done. "Fine words butter no parsnips," "Silence is golden," and "Talk is cheap" are other old sayings about the subject of too much talk and not enough action.

There is, however, a long tradition in Ireland of admiring the fluent and the witty person, and Irish people have a reputation as good talkers the world over. Storytelling, which had been for centuries the main source of entertainment around the fire at night, was dealt a deathblow by the advent of television in the early sixties. When a person, whether young or old, visited a neighbor's house, he or she was expected to have a story to tell. There is a proverb that says, "Tell a story, compose a lie, or get out" (*Inis scéal, cum breág, nó bí amuigh*). In my youth this proverb tended to be taken seriously in Irish-speaking areas, and children, from a very young age, had a repertoire of stories. There were even stories about people who did not have a story to tell when they happened into a strange house and were penalized for their shortcoming.

Asking for silver.

124

Molann an obair an fear.

The work praises the man.

Making a currach, Connemara, Co. Galway

Is é an bia capall na hoibre.

Food is a good workhorse.

By 1845, the year of the Great Famine, Ireland had reached its point of greatest dependence on the potato. Before this vegetable was introduced, at the end of the sixteenth century, the population relied mainly on grain and milk as its principal foods. Cheese making had been widespread, but this practice died out in the eighteenth century. Butter, however, retained its popularity and has always been eaten in enormous quantities in Ireland. In medieval times, from the mid-twelfth to the mid-sixteenth centuries, it was often flavored with garlic or onions.

The Irish diet, with milk and grain as the staple foods, remained relatively unchanged until the introduction of the potato. The potato was first brought to Europe from the New World in 1588, and tradition as well as some historical evidence links the name of Sir Walter Raleigh with its introduction to Ireland. The potato solved Ireland's food problems for a long period but was an unreliable crop, as the Great Famine was to prove, when potato blight ruined the crop in successive years.

Grain has been grown in Ireland since Neolithic times (4000–2000 B.C.), when saddle querns were used for grinding it. Simple water mills, known as horizontal mills, were in use as early as the seventh century. Oats, barley, wheat, and rye were the types of grain eaten, mainly as porridge and bread. Porridge, which is still popular, was

not exclusively a breakfast food then but was eaten in large quantities, hot or cold, at all times of the day, with milk, buttermilk, or sour milk.

Fishing was popular in Ireland in the medieval period, and although large quantities of fish were exported to England and the Continent, the mackerel in great shoals only made its appearance in Irish coastal waters in the second half of the nineteenth century. (Timothy O'Neill, *Life and Tradition in Rural Ireland*).

Potatoes—the workhorse.

Mura gcuirfidh tú san earrach ní bhainfidh tú san fhómhar.

If you do not sow in the spring you will not reap in the autumn.

Digging the potatoes.

129

Terry's (Mc Donagh's) Bar, Rossaveal, Connemara, Co. Galway.

Drink
Ól

"What butter or whiskey does not cure cannot be cured" (*An rud nach leigheasann im ná uisce beatha níl aon leigheas air*) is a proverb that leaves no doubt about the esteem in which whiskey (*uisce beatha*, water of life, *aqua vitae*) was held by many of our ancestors. *Fuisce,* a corruption of "whiskey," is the name still given in many parts of the west of Ireland to homemade, illicitly distilled whiskey, more commonly known nowadays as "poteen" (*poitín*). To distinguish between the legal and the illicit spirits, the legal commodity is called "shop whiskey" (*fuisce siopa*).

In the last century many boats (Galway Hookers, as they are now called) from Connemara made the journey to Guernsey, one of the Channel Islands between England and France, which was exempt from tax. They bought brandy, rum, and the best of wines at a very low price and brought them home to Connemara where they were sold at an enormous profit to the wealthy few who could afford them. The British government's coast guard ships, known as "the king's cutters," were always on the lookout for smugglers and ready to give chase. Many a fine boat, complete with its valuable cargo, was captured and confiscated and its owner fined heavily or imprisoned. Daring and memorable escapes occurred, some of which are immortalized in traditional songs that are still very popular.

One such escape gave its name to Brandy Harbor, in Connemara, where a local smuggler put his cargo of Guernsey brandy ashore after being pursued by one of the king's cutters. He cunningly eluded the coast guards by suddenly turning off the main channel, pulling alongside a steep cliff, lowering his sails, and putting his cargo to one side of the boat so that his mast lay close against the cliff face and was not noticeable to the enemy in pursuit.

Is túisce deoch ná scéal.

A drink precedes a story.

Although storytelling has nearly disappeared in Ireland, this proverb is still very popular among Irish speakers, and it is generally quoted by the woman or man of the house while giving a welcoming drink to a friend or visitor. To evoke the proverb gives a certain dignity to the occasion and makes everyone feel that to have a drink is the right thing to do.

The group in the photograph is very much in the spirit of the proverb. The picture was taken in 1957 in Seán Ó Confhaola's Public House on Inisheer (*Inis Oírr*), one of the Aran Islands, and shows Leo Corduff, from the Irish Folklore Department in University College Dublin, about to record folklore from a group of islanders.

According to tradition, drink was invented by the Devil as a device to part people from God, and many stories are told linking the Devil and drink. One such story tells of Saint Patrick visiting a tavern in West Kerry and calling for a pint. The woman went to the barrel, drew the pint, and handed it to him. Saint Patrick asked her to fill it all the way up. She put another drop into it but it was not yet full. He had to ask her three times before it was full. "Look over to your right," said Saint Patrick to her. She did, and she saw a huge, fat dog on top of the barrel. The dog, of course, was the Devil who was thriving on the ill-gotten gains of the dishonest tavern woman. At the end of a year and a day, Saint Patrick passed that way again and went into the same tavern and called for a pint. The woman filled the pint up to the brim. "Did you fill each pint like that during the year?" Saint Patrick asked her. She said she did. "Look over to your right," said Saint Patrick. As she did, she saw a small dog whose bones were sticking out through his skin, walking to and fro on top of the barrel.

Stories like this one were used by preachers as examples, their purpose being to warn against dishonesty.

Seán Ó Confhaola's Public House, Inisheer, Aran Islands.

Leigheas na póite a hól arís.

The cure for the hangover is to drink again.

Poteen (*poitín*) is still being made in many parts of Ireland in more or less the same fashion as it was a hundred years ago. The only big difference is that bottled gas has replaced the turf fire, and this has made detection by the police (*gardaí*) much more difficult.

To make the whiskey, bags of barley are submerged in water for two days until the grain is swollen. The bags are then taken out and covered with old sacks or some other available material. As the water drains out of the bags and the covering provides protection from the cold and light, the grain begins to germinate. The bags are emptied, and the grain is spread out evenly on a dry floor and turned a few times a day until it has fully dried. The grain is then hardened over the heat of a fire, a process that used to be done in a special kiln (*áith*) but is now done with bottled gas.

The hardened, swollen grain, which tastes very sweet at this stage, is ground into meal or malt (*braich*) and placed in a large wooden barrel, where water that is almost boiling is poured over it. When it cools, the liquid, known as "wort" (*braichlis*), is drained into a separate barrel while more hot water (boiling water this second time) is applied to the malt to make more wort. When the lukewarm wort is in a barrel or barrels of its own, some baker's yeast is applied to cause fermentation and the mixture is allowed to ferment for a minimum of two or three days, after which it is ready for the still.

The heat under the pot causes the alcohol vapor to rise and pass through the "arm" and through the "worm," a coil of copper piping that is placed in a barrel of cold water. As the vapor passes through the cold copper piping, it condenses, and the resulting liquid is known as "singling" (*singleáil*). This liquid is collected and "doubled" (sent through the still again), and the liquid that comes through the worm the second time is genuine Irish traditional whiskey or *poitín*.

Poteen still.

134

Policemen destroying poteen still.

135

Dá fheabhas é an t-ól is é an tart a dheireadh.

Good as drink is, it ends in thirst.

An eighteenth-century Ulster poet, Cathal Buí Mac Giolla Ghunna (*buí* means "yellow"), who was very fond of the drink, was moved to poetry on seeing a bird known as *an bonnán buí* (the yellow bittern) lying dead on the ice of a frozen pond, having died of thirst. Fearing a similar fate for himself, the poet advises everybody to drink while they can, as there will not be a drop to be had after death:

My wife asked me to give up the drink,
That I would only live a very short while.
I said unto her that she was a liar,
That getting that drink would lengthen my life.
Don't you see the bird of the easy throat
That died of thirst a while ago
And neighbours of my heart let you wet your
 mouth
Because you won't get a drop after your death.

The juice of the barley would lift the fog off
 you,
O God of glory in heaven above!
In the public houses every Sunday night
It is my sustenance, my drink and my bite
It is a pity that I don't get it always
Every moment of night and day.
And you, young people who are unmarried
Let you be drinking or your lives will be short.

(Translated from the Irish)

Naughton's Pub, Galway.

136

Conroy-Coyne's Bar, Kilkerrin, Connemara, Co. Galway.

137

Seachain teach an tabhairne nó is bairnigh is beatha duit.

Beware of the public house or limpets will be your food.

A pint of Guinness, Kenmare, Co. Kerry.

Nuair a bhíos an braon istigh bíonn an chiall amuigh.

When the drop is inside the sense is outside.

Drinking Guinness in the pub

Nuair a d'imigh an leann d'imigh an greann.

When the liquor was gone the fun was gone.

Irish men have a reputation for being easily enticed into a public house. A common excuse is to say that the work being done is "thirsty work" and to adjourn for a few drinks. Séamus Murphy, the sculptor and author, believed that stonecutting was the thirstiest work of all, and in his book, *Stone Mad,* he tells of the frequent visits of the "stonies" to the local pub. He describes the irresistible urge to buy a round of drinks for one's friends:

The "thrill"—that is the inclination "to stand" to all and sundry—used to be discussed very objectively. "All of a sudden it came over me and although I knew I was doing the eejit I stood to the lot of them, saying to hell with poverty, and feeling a big fella."

On such occasions, when a man feels the thrill coming over him he starts off by asking a couple of men in for a drink. The rest spot it and in a few minutes they are all in. . . .

A regular ritual is observed. One of the "Dust" opens the pub door for him and lets him through. He walks straight to the counter while all the rest remain a discreet distance behind him. Then he turns and says: "What is it?" Pints usually, and one by one the men move up to the counter and claim their drinks and somebody will play up to him by reminding him of some epic with which he was connected. These sorts of events end in a sing-song:

"Happy are we all together,
Happy are we one and all,
May we live a life of pleasure,
May we never, never die."

In Dwyer's Pub, Leeson Street, Dublin.

O'Flaherty's Bar, Costelloe, Connemara, Co. Galway.

141

Is milis dá ól é ach is searbh dá íoc é.

It is sweet to drink but bitter to pay for.

Paying for the drink.

Is é an tart deireadh an óil agus is é an brón deireadh na meisce.

Thirst is the end of drinking and sorrow is the end of drunkenness.

O'Neill's Pub, Tara Street, Dublin.

Dónall ar meisce agus a bhean ag ól uisce.

Dónall drunk and his wife drinking water.

Terry's (Mc Donagh's) Bar, Rossaveal, Connemara, Co. Galway.

Sceitheann fíon fírinne.

Wine divulges truth.

"The wine of the country" is what James Joyce called Guinness, the dark ale with the creamy head that is known far and wide as the Irish national drink. The first Arthur Guinness founded his brewery in Dublin in 1759, and before the end of the nineteenth century it had become the largest brewery in the world. It is still the largest in Europe.

A fleet of barges, carrying Guinness for export, plied the river between brewery and port. The first export shipment of Guinness—six and one-half barrels—left the port of Dublin in 1769 on a sailing ship, part of a regular shipping line bound for England. That first modest trickle soon became a profitable flood—so much so that by 1913 Guinness needed a ship of its own solely for the purpose of handling Guinness exports.

When the Grand Canal, linking Dublin with the River Shannon, opened in 1798, roads were virtually nonexistent outside

Guinness's barge on the River Liffey.

Dublin. So the canal provided a great boost to business, opening up the first viable trade route between the capital and the South and West, via the Shannon. The first barge to travel the route carried a cargo of Guinness. So did the last, when the canal finally closed in 1961 (replaced by more efficient road and rail transport), and these old Guinness barges are still remembered with affection by Dubliners.

Guinness's Brewery, Dublin, at the turn of the century.

145

Cill Rialaigh, Co. Kerry.

Hereditary Nature
Dúchas

Seán Ó Conaill's Book is a translation by Máire Mac Neill of *Leabhar Sheáin Í Chonaill,* a collection of stories, legends, and miscellaneous items of tradition. They were written down by Professor Séamus Ó Duilearga (James Hamilton Delargy) and were told by the outstanding storyteller Seán Ó Conaill, a farmer from Cill Rialaigh, Co. Kerry, about fourteen miles from Caherciveen.

The first folktale in this famous book tells of the origin of the cat, the animal most often mentioned in proverbs about hereditary nature. The making of the cat was very much a case of "necessity being the mother of invention" (*múineann gá seift*). Saint Martin, whose feast day falls on November 11, had a hand in it, as shall be seen from the story. (Until very recently it was customary to kill an animal on the feast of Saint Martin, a custom that is linked with an earlier tradition of killing and salting farm animals after autumn, in order to supply food through the winter and spring.)

According to the story, the origin of pigs, mice, rats, and cats is as follows:

From St. Martin's fat they were made. He was travelling around, and one night he came to a house and yard. At that time there were only cattle; there were no pigs or piglets. He asked the man of the house if there was anything to eat the chaff and the grain. The man replied there were only the cattle. St. Martin said it was a great pity to have that much chaff going to waste. At night when they were going to bed, he handed a piece of fat to the servant-girl and told her to put it under a tub turned upside down, and not to look at it at all until he would give her the word next day. The girl did so, but she kept a bit of the fat, and put it under a keeler to find out what it would be.

When St. Martin rose next day he asked her if she had looked under the tub. She said she had not. He told her to go and lift up the tub. She lifted it up, and there under it were a sow and twelve piglets. It was a great wonder to them, as they had never before seen pig or piglet.

The girl then went to the keeler and lifted it, and it was full of mice and rats! As soon as the keeler was lifted, they went running about the house searching for any hole they could go into. When St. Martin saw them, he pulled off one of his mittens and threw it at them and made a cat with that throw. And that is why the cat ever since goes after mice and rats.

Seán Ó Conaill in 1930.

147

Briseann an dúchas trí shúile an chait.

Nature breaks through the eyes of the cat.

The following piece from *Seán Ó Conaill's Book* is an example of the storyteller's method of explaining the meaning of proverbs:

There was a farmer who had a cat, and every night the cat used to hold the light for him when he was eating his supper. He was very proud of owning this cat, and used to talk about it to everyone, and wager with anyone who would take him up on it.

One night a poor scholar came in, and at supper-time the cat went to the head of the table, took the light, and held it between its two paws until they had finished the meal. The farmer asked the poor scholar if he had ever before seen a cat do such work. He replied he had not. The farmer said he would lay a bet with him that whatever the cat might see, it would mind the light during the meal. The poor scholar said it would not. So each of them wagered five pounds, but the poor scholar asked for a stay until he came that way again.

After a short while the poor scholar returned, and he had three live mice in a box in his pocket. Now, said he to the farmer, they would test the cat that night.

When the food was ready it was put on the table. The cat went on top, and held the candle between its two front paws. They were eating then, and the cat was holding the light. The poor scholar put his hand behind him, pulled out the box, and let one mouse out across the table. The cat fixed its two eyes on it with a fierce look but did not move. He did the same thing a second time, and there was not a limb of the cat that did not quiver. He released the third mouse, and the cat threw the candle, and went after the mouse.

The poor scholar won the wager; and then he asked the farmer if he had ever heard that "nature breaks out through the eyes of the cat."

McDonagh's kitchen, Kilronan, Aran Islands.

149

Céard a dhéanfadh mac an chait ach luch a mharú?

What would the cat's son do but kill a mouse?

This Old Irish poem, titled "The Monk and his Pet Cat," was written by an anonymous poet and translated by Robin Flower:

I and Pangur Bán, my cat,
'Tis a like task we are at;
Hunting mice is his delight,
Hunting words I sit all night.

Better far than praise of men
'Tis to sit with book and pen;
Pangur bears me no ill will,
He too plies his simple skill.

'Tis a merry thing to see
At our tasks how glad are we,
When at home we sit and find
Entertainment to our mind.

Oftentimes a mouse will stray
In the hero Pangur's way;
Oftentimes my keen thought set
Takes a meaning in its net.

'Gainst the wall he sets his eye
Full and fierce and sharp and sly;
'Gainst the wall of knowledge I
All my little wisdom try.

When a mouse darts from its den,
O how glad is Pangur then!
O what gladness do I prove
When I solve the doubts I love!

So in peace our tasks we ply,
Pangur Bán, my cat, and I;
In our arts we find our bliss,
I have mine and he has his.

Practice every day has made
Pangur perfect in his trade;
I get wisdom day and night
Turning darkness into light.

Mar a bhíos an cú mór a bhíos an coileán.

As the big hound is, so will the pup be.

A March Cock.

Drochubh, drochéan.

A bad egg, a bad bird.

It was widely believed that the crowing of the cock had supernatural powers to ward off evil spirits. A cock that was hatched in the month of March out of an egg that was laid in March was called a March Cock (*Coileach Márta*) and was believed to have exceptional powers against evil spirits. The old people maintained, however, that a March Cock had to come from parents that were hatched in March from eggs laid in March, and still others maintained that a *real* March Cock had to come from a line of seven sets of parents, all hatched in March from eggs laid in March.

It was believed in parts of rural Ireland, well into this century, that evil spirits skulked in the night and were only dispelled by the crowing of the cock in the early morning. When people had to leave the house very early in the morning, they generally made sure that the cock had crowed three times before they did so.

As may be expected, *Seán Ó Conaill's Book* contains a tale about a March Cock:

Long ago there was a coal-ship lying by the quay in some harbour. During the night the captain went up on deck, and he saw a black cloud in the sky approaching him. He stayed watching it until it came down on a house at the edge of the harbour, and as soon as it came to the house the cock crowed and it went away. Next day the captain came to the woman of the house and asked her if she would sell the cock, and offered her seven shillings and sixpence, but she would not sell.

That night again the captain went on deck the same way, and saw the cloud coming again. He stayed watching it until it descended on the house, and no sooner was that done than the cock crowed. The cloud went away then.

The captain came again to the woman of the house next morning, and asked her if she would sell the cock, and she said she would not; but he offered her fifteen shillings and sixpence, and she gave it to him.

The captain stayed the third night watching, and he saw the cloud come again and descending on the house, and no sooner was that done than the house went on fire.

Cuir síoda ar ghabhar agus is gabhar i gcónaí é.

Put silk on a goat and it is still a goat.

"You cannot make a silk purse out of a sow's ear."

The goat, like the donkey, has a very low standing in the animal world, and to be compared to a goat can be very insulting. The legendary origin of the goat, as given in *Seán Ó Conaill's Book*, may help us to understand why this is so:

It was the Devil who invented the goat because he thought that he himself could create something as well as God. He made the goat, but if he did, he could not put life into it. Then when Our Saviour saw it made, he said that it might serve mankind, and he put life into it. But its milk has no cream, unlike the sheep's. The sheep is nobler and more worthy of honour: it makes clothing for day and night for the people.

The hair of the goat, or mohair, is in popular demand nowadays, however, as is goat's milk and cheese. Goat's milk is widely believed to contain curative, if not supernatural, qualities and the poet Patrick Kavanagh (1905–1968) was aware of this when he wrote this poem titled "The Goat of Slieve Donard," which is found in his *Collected Poems:*

I saw an old white goat on the slope of Slieve
    Donard
Nibbling daintily at the herb leaves that grow in
    the crevasses,
And I thought of James Stephens—
He wrote of an old white goat within my
    remembering,
Seven years ago I read—
Now it comes back
Full of the dreaming black beautiful crags.
I shall drink of the white goat's milk,
The old white goat of Slieve Donard,
Slieve Donard where the herbs of wisdom
    grow,
The herbs of the Secret of Life that the old
    white goat has nibbled,
And I shall live longer than Methuselah,
Brother to no man.

Goats at The Burren, Co. Clare.

Is treise dúchas ná oiliúint.

Instinct is stronger than upbringing.

Irish proverbs frequently refer to the strong instinctive nature with which animals care for and protect their young. Liam O'Flaherty (1896–1984) uses this instinct to great effect in his short story, "The Blow." Here we meet a hard, rough, nineteenth-century gombeen man as he is buying bonhams (piglets) from a neighbor. He is accompanied by his young son, Nedeen, who, in his father's eyes, is a weakling. The man roars abuse at the boy and, what hurts the young lad most of all, insults the mother the boy loves so dearly. "There's not a drop of my blood in you," the father screams. "After your mother you took, you aimless, lazy, useless thing you."

The father shows the boy how all the bonhams but one are freely suckled by the sow lying on her flank for them to reach her paps. The one exception is cruelly and derisively pointed out to the boy by the father as a weakling, jostled from the paps by the stronger bonhams, even kicked by the sow. The boy protests that the sow loves its young. The father strikes him, but the boy takes it in such a silent, unflinching, terrible anger that the father is shamed and frightened, and slinks away. A few moments later the boy hears the sow again squealing, but this time he knows it is for the one missing bonham who races for her breast and is freely fed. At this a sudden inrush of warm tenderness transfers itself from beast to boy, and from boy to father. Looking down at the sow and its weakling bonham the boy weeps because "love has returned again to earth" (Seán O Faoláin, *The Pleasures of Gaelic Literature*).

Mare and her foal.

An té a bhíos fial roinneann Dia leis.

God shares with the person who is generous.

Sharing in a Dublin street.

Is minic duine bocht fiúntach.

A poor person is often worthy.

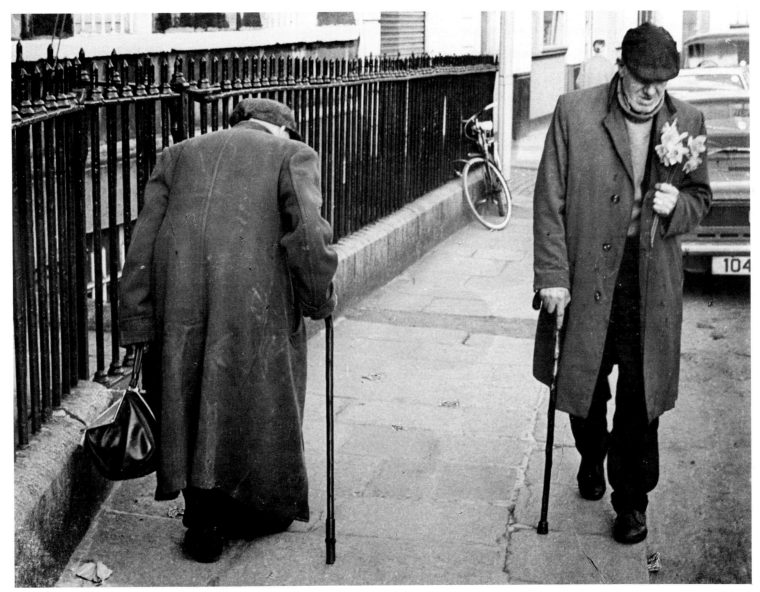

Mother's Day in Dublin, 1976.

An bairille a mbíonn an fíon ann, fanann an braon sna cláir.

The barrel that contains the wine will retain the drop in its staves.

This proverb is quoted when a parent's good trait manifests itself in a daughter or a son.

Old wine and whiskey barrels were much sought after well into the first half of this century to reuse their staves to make churns, as these staves gave a special flavor to the butter.

Coopering (barrel-making) has been practiced in Ireland since the early Christian period, but it did not reach its height until the middle of the nineteenth century. The Romans brought the craft to England, and it was brought from there to Ireland. It was also practiced in ancient Egypt.

In the eighteenth and nineteenth centuries in Ireland, distillers, brewers, butter merchants, and butchers employed coopers to make all sorts of barrels, casks, and containers. A hogshead of whiskey held fifty-five gallons, whereas a hogshead of brandy held sixty gallons, and a brewer's hogshead held fifty-two gallons. For the farming community the coopers made churns, tubs, piggins, noggins, buckets, cools for gathering milk, washing tubs, and a variety of other vessels.

Coopering calls for a skill for instinctive measurement rarely required in other crafts.

Without any written measurements, the cooper must produce vessels of symmetrical proportions that will hold precise weights and measures. Each vessel must be strong enough to withstand the pounding of the dash in a churn or the pressure of fermenting liquids, and it must last a lifetime and endure rough handling.

The coopering trade began to die out in the present century with the spread of creameries, and the advent of cheap plastic materials sounded its death knell. Just as the tinsmith has become obsolete, so the cooper's craft is no longer needed, though coopers are still employed in the distilleries in Bushmills in Co. Antrim and in Midleton in Co. Cork.

In David Shaw-Smith's excellent book, *Ireland's Traditional Crafts*, Timothy O'Neill bemoans the passing of a great craft:

We lose a part of our history and our heritage with the death of a craft just as surely as with the loss of architectural remains. The curiosity of Ireland is that the disappearance of a craft generates little sense of loss and this lack of awareness is typical of our neglect of our material folk heritage.

Is minic nach ndeachaigh bó le bó dhúchais.

It is often a cow does not take after its breed.

Food and light.

Hidden Meaning
Ciall Faoi Cheilt

One of the many pleasant memories of my early youth in Connemara is of spending the long summer holidays in my grandparents' thatched cottage on the side of a mountain, a few miles from our family home. Although our grandfather made all of us children work hard every day, usually on the bog, I always looked forward to sitting by the fireside at dusk, listening to the cricket behind the hob, and watching the long shadows dance between the dresser and the fire.

The paraffin lamp, which was the source of light in most rural houses at the time, was never lit until it was quite dark, and there was always a certain ceremony about lighting it. A thin strip of bog deal was usually used to carry the flame from the fire to the lamp wick. After allowing some time for the globe to absorb the heat, the wick was turned up fully, dispelling all shadows and filling the house with a gentle yellow light. At that magical moment my grandfather always uttered the following saying: "Woe to whoever ate or drank the light's portion" (*Mairg a d'ith nó a d'ól cuid an tsolais*).

When, in later life, I tried to find out the origin of that old saying nobody seemed to know, not even those who remembered hearing it. You can imagine my surprise and delight, therefore, a few short years ago while visiting a house in a neighboring parish, on hearing the man of the house, Seán Bheairtle Ó Mainín, utter the same old saying while lighting his paraffin lamp. Better still, he told me the origin of it. It dates back to the time when poor people had to depend for light on the fat or grease of animals or fowl, melted in a sea-shell. As this fat and grease also made very tasty sauce with their staple diet of potatoes, there was always a strong temptation to eat or drink it instead of saving it for the light. The old saying served both as an incentive for saving the "light's portion" and as a celebration for having done so. One is reminded of the above proverb when reading one of Liam O'Flaherty's short stories, *The Pedlar's Revenge*, in which the peddler kills his half-starved lifelong enemy by tricking him into melting candles on a frying pan and eating potatoes fried in the molten wax.

House in Casla, Connemara, Co. Galway.

As a ceann a bhlitear an bhó.

The cow is milked from her head.

The food that is put under a cow's head will determine the amount of milk she will give, which explains the literal meaning of the proverb. Like all good proverbs, there are metaphorical connotations as well. Recently, while watching a certain journalist wine and dine a person from whom he hoped to get a good story, a colleague of mine turned to me and quoted the above proverb in Irish. The notion of "milking" (*bleán*) somebody for a story is quite common in Irish, and the wining and dining suitably provided the other element of the proverb. It was very apt.

There are many superstitions about cows and their milk. It was widely believed, when a cow kicked over the milking vessel and spilled the milk, that the fairies wanted the milk, and the expression, "It was needed where it went" (*Theastaigh sé san áit a ndeachaigh sé*), is still common in Irish-speaking areas when milk is spilled.

The sign of the cross on the cow's udder was one of the many ways of protecting the milk, and the tradition still exists, after milking, of dipping one's thumb in the fresh milk's froth and making the sign of the cross on the cow's hindquarter with it. Certain women were believed to have the power of bewitching the milk from a neighbor's cow and of bewitching the butter off a neighbor's churning. A cow, while calving, was very susceptible to having its beestings (early milk) stolen by a neighboring witch, and in

order to prevent this happening, a piece of cow dung was immediately placed in the newborn calf's mouth. Until very recently, red embers from the open fire were placed, for protection, under milk churns, and a loop of rowan or a piece of red cloth or thread was tied around the cows' tails on May Day, a date traditionally associated with the fairies.

Inishmaan (Inis Meáin, Middle Island), Co. Galway.

Éist le fuaim na habhann agus gheobhaidh tú breac.

Listen to the sound of the river and you will get a trout.

Fishing in the Costelloe River (Abhainn Chasla), Connemara, Co. Galway.

Bíonn grásta Dé idir an diallait agus an talamh.

The grace of God is found between the saddle and the ground.

Many Irish religious legends tell of the hope of a soul in Purgatory that it will be released through a Mass to be said by a priest, as yet unborn. The idea of a soul doing Purgatory in a river is quite common in such legends.

The following, from Seán O'Sullivan's *Legends from Ireland*, is called "Twixt Saddle and Ground":

There was a man long ago, and a long time ago it was. If I were there then, I wouldn't be there now. I'd have a new story or an old story, or maybe I'd be without any story! This man was doing every kind of badness, and stealing and robbing. One day he was riding his horse by the side of a river. The sun shone for a moment, and the rider heard someone laughing. He drew up his horse and caught sight of a person. "Why are you laughing?" asked the rider. The man who had laughed was standing in the current of the river. "Last night a baby boy was born to my grandson, and he'll be a priest later on. The first Mass he will celebrate will release me from here." "How long have you been here?" asked the rider. "Twenty years next Easter Sunday." "What sins have you committed?" "When I was young," said the man in the river, "I mocked and made fun of everybody and had little pity for those who were afflicted." "Well," said the rider, "I have no chance at all of saving my soul!" He dismounted in order to take his stand in the river. And between the stirrup and the ground his sins were forgiven, as he had examined his conscience and submitted to what was in store for him.

Twixt saddle and ground
Mercy he asked for, mercy found.

I gcosa con a bhíos a chuid.

A hound's food is in its legs.

The hound has long depended on its speed for its food, and conversely, the better the food the hound gets, the faster it can run. Coursing the hare has been a very popular pastime in Ireland for centuries, and the Irish greyhound is nearly as world-famous as the Irish horse. Most coursing meetings are held in park enclosures where the hares are trained to run up the field toward an escape through which the dogs cannot follow. In recent years, however, coursing events in which the greyhounds are allowed to savage the hare have been the cause of much controversy and heated protest. Irish dogs, from the famous Master McGrath of a century ago, to Full Pete, Dubedoon, and Kentucky Minstrel in more recent times, have added to the prestige of the Irish greyhound by frequently winning the major English coursing event, the Waterloo Cup, run near Liverpool each year.

Ireland's first two greyhound-racing tracks were opened in Belfast and in Dublin in 1927 and since then Irish dogs have been just as successful at chasing the mechanical hares as they had been at chasing the live ones. There are more than twenty licensed greyhound tracks in the country at the moment, the majority of them in the Republic, and breeding of greyhounds for track racing has become a major industry. The world's largest greyhound sales are held in Dublin, and the supremacy of the Irish greyhound is now well established.

There is hardly a follower of the sport who has not heard of the legendary Mick the Miller from the Irish Midlands, who won the English Derby twice and finished first on a third occasion, only to be beaten on a rerun. Between 1920 and 1932 he won nineteen races in succession and nine thousand pounds in prize money. Spanish Battleship came out of Kerry in the fifties to win the Irish Derby three times in a row and another Kerry-born dog, Balyregan Bob, set a world record recently by winning thirty-two races in a row.

Coursing the hare.

170

I gcosa duine a bhíos a shláinte.

A person's health is in his feet.

There was a belief in Ireland that a man caught a cold through a wetting of the feet, and a woman caught a cold through a wetting of the head, which gives the above proverb a strong leaning toward male chauvinism. Until very recently, young boys and girls in some rural areas wore shoes or boots only in winter and spring and went barefooted during the rest of the year except, possibly, when going to Mass on Sunday. Even then, those who lived in remote areas would only put their shoes on when they were very near the church in order to save them from wear.

The Aran Islands in Galway Bay are the only places where homemade footwear is still made from raw cowhide. These shoes

Bartley Flaherty baiting his spillet for fishing, Inishmaan, Aran Islands, Co. Galway.

are called *bróga úrleathair* (rawhide shoes) in Irish and "pampooties" in English, and they were at one time made of sealskin. The shoes have no heel, and the hairy side of the hide is worn on the outside. Each pampootie is made from a single piece of cowhide that has been cured by rubbing salt into it. The foot is placed on the hide and an oblong section is cut out, large enough to be folded around the foot. A leather thong or some similar cord is threaded through the hide, laced over the toes, and gripped at the back of the heel. After the pampooties are made,

the hide is rolled up and stored until the next pair is needed. Pampooties are very suitable for walking on the sharp limestone rocks of Aran that would quickly ruin a pair of conventional shoes. They are ideal for clambering in and out of the frail canvas-covered currach, and can get wet frequently without coming to any harm, as they dry out very soon in the sun or wind. If they are allowed to become hard they will hurt the feet, so they are often soaked in a bucket of water overnight or dunked in the sea during the day to keep the leather supple.

Pampooties.

Tiocfaidh an lá fós a mbeidh gnó ag an mbó dá heireaball.

The day will yet come when the cow will have use for her tail.

"There are better days ahead."

Is fada an bóthar nach mbíonn casadh ann.

It is a long road that has no turning.

"Every cloud has a silver lining."

Kinvara (Cinn Mhara), Connemara, Co. Galway.

Feileann spallaí do bhallaí chomh maith le clocha móra.

Spalds (small stones) suit walls as well as big stones.

Just as the big stones in a wall are propped up and kept in place by the smaller stones, so are the well-off members of society propped up and kept in place by the less well-off. In a country where successive generations have devoted so much time and energy to the building of thousands and thousands of miles of stone walls, it is not surprising to find these walls immortalized in one of our proverbs.

Séamus Murphy (1907–1975), the Irish sculptor, in his beautiful book, *Stone Mad*, tells of his life as a stonecutter and of the many "stonies" he had known in the trade. One of the most colorful of these was a journeyman stonecutter called Black Jack, who had the reputation of being the greatest walker in Ireland, and who was full of stories about his experiences on the roads. He tells this story of a day he was passing near a farmhouse, and a man put his head over the ditch:

"Good morning," said the man. "Good morning," said I. And the day being fine and I with nothing to do, we talked about this, that and the other. Eventually he wormed me occupation out of me, and when I said I was a stonecutter, "You áre the very man I want," said he. "Come up to the house and I'll show you what I want you to do." So up I went and to my astonishment the job was to castrate a boar! So that was his notion of a stonecutter. Of course when I saw the way the wind blew I held tough and promised to attend to the business in the morning. I had a good dinner out of him and then he put me up in the barn. I slept well but I didn't wait for the cocks to call me. I was off before sunrise, wondering how any man could be so stupid and so ignorant of the oldest of all the crafts. "Blast it," said I, "didn't we do the most important of all jobs? Didn't we cut the Ten Commandments on the slabs of Moses? And to think that I would live to see the day when a bostoon of a farmer would take me for a vet!"

Stone wall on Inishmaan.

Baist do leanbh féin ar dtús.

Baptize your own child first.

By this is meant, "Attend to your own affairs first before troubling about other people's." It is sometimes said as an excuse for serving oneself first. Another version of the proverb is, "The priest baptizes his own child first" (*Baisteann an sagart a leanbh féin ar dtús*). An account of the origin of the proverb is given in Seán O'Sullivan's *Legends from Ireland:*

There was a poor man there long ago. He and his wife had a big family. He said that he would leave her for seven years. He came back after the seven years, and nine months later his wife gave birth to seven children in one "round." The father then said that he would drown them. He put them into a basket, and took it on his back to drown them. On the road he met a priest who asked him what he had in the basket. He said he had little pups. The priest didn't believe him and told him to let down the basket to see what was in it. When he did this, the priest saw the seven baby boys and told the father that he should be ashamed to do such a thing. The man said that he couldn't help it, he had no means of rearing them.

Then the priest baptized the first one, and said that he would keep him for himself. He baptized the others too and sent them to be reared by six priests. When the seven grew up, they all became priests. The Seven Churches in Lough Derg are named after them. They say that's a true story, any way!

The legend of the seven babies who were saved from drowning and later became bishops was popular in many parts of Ireland. Many old ecclesiastical centers exist where seven churches stood in former centuries.

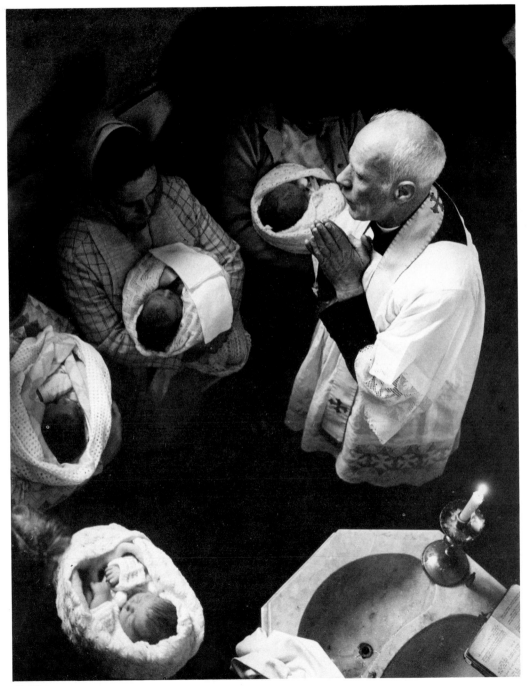

Baptism.

Rocks in Connemara.

Nuair a chuirtear tine leis an gcloch pléascann sí.

When fire is applied to the stone it cracks.

"We all have our breaking point."

Fire and rocks.

Casla, Connemara, Co. Galway.

Miscellaneous Proverbs

Inishmaan, Aran Islands.

Níl aon dlí ar an riachtanas.

Necessity knows no law.

Saint Patrick's Day scene, Dublin

Múineann gá seift.

Need teaches a plan.

"Necessity is the mother of invention."

Public transport, Rathlin Island, off Co. Antrim, 1960.

Is minic a crochadh duine gan seift.

Lack of resource has hanged many a person.

Coming home from the creamery, West Cork.

Ag duine féin is fearr a fhios cá luíonn an bhróg air.

The wearer best knows where the shoe pinches.

Temporary relief, Dublin.

Meileann muilte Dé go mall ach meileann siad go mín.

The mills of God grind slowly but they grind finely.

Mill wheel, near Nanagh, Co. Tipperary.

Níl tuile nach dtránn ach tuile na ngrás.

Every tide has an ebb save the tide of graces.

Saying the Rosary on Inishmaan, Aran Islands.

Is gaire cabhair Dé ná an doras.

God's help is nearer than the door.

Mass time on Inishmaan, Aran Islands.

D'ordaigh Dia cúnamh.

God ordered help.

Spraying potatoes against blight, Inishmaan, Aran Islands.

Ní bhíonn an rath ach mar a mbíonn an smacht.

There is no luck except where there is discipline.

Waiting for the "steamer," Kilronan, Inishmore, Aran Islands.

Bí go maith leis an ngarlach agus tiocfaidh sé amárach.

Be good to the child and he will come to you tomorrow.

Rossaveal (Ros a'Mhíl) National School, Connemara, Co. Galway.

Is maith an rud grá nó faitíos.

Love or fear is a great thing.

After the Saint Patrick's Day Parade, Dublin.

An beagán, go minic, a fhágas roic sa sparán.

A little, often, leaves wrinkles in the purse.

Money changing hands, Galway.

Aíne Ní Cheallaigh in Ballyconneely, Connemara, Co. Galway.

Is trom cearc i bhfad.

A hen is heavy when carried far.

A present of a hen, Connemara, Co. Galway.

Is onóraí poll ná paiste.

A hole is more honorable than a patch.

Art on the Quays, Dublin.

Is maith an scéalaí an aimsir.

Time is a great storyteller.

Halloween Divination, Connemara, Co. Galway. Divination has been a popular pastime at Halloween. The girl in the photograph is trying to find out if she will marry (ring), cross the sea (water), or die young (clay).

200

Is gliobach í an chearc go dtógann sí a hál.

The hen has ruffled feathers until she rears her brood.

Hen with chicks.

Coming home from the creamery, across the strand, in Ballyferriter, Co. Kerry.

202

Mair a chapaill agus gheobhaidh tú féar.

Live, horse and you will get grass.

Near Dingle, Co. Kerry.

Kilronan, Inishmore, Aran Islands.

Is ceirín do gach créacht an fhoighne.

Patience is a poultice for all wounds.

O'Connell Street, Dublin, with O'Connell monument in the background.

204

Ní heaspa go díth carad.

There is no need like the lack of a friend.

Alone, Stephen's Green, Dublin.

Is cuma le fear na mbróg cá leagann sé a chos.

The man with the boots does not mind where he places his foot.

A day out in Killorglin, Co. Kerry.

Maireann croí éadrom i bhfad.

A light heart lives long.

Roadside dancing, Co. Carlow.

Luggage on the beach in Inishmaan, Aran Islands.

An áit a bhfuil do chroí is ann a thabharfas do chosa thú.

Your feet will bring you to where your heart is.

Thatched cottage, Inishmaan, Aran Islands.

Quotation Proverbs

The most humorous Irish proverbs by far are those known as "quotation proverbs." They not only lack the seriousness and solemnity of ordinary proverbs, but they turn some of them about and hold them up to ridicule: "'There is no luck except where there is discipline'—as the son said while beating his father" ("*Ní bhíonn an rath ach mar a mbíonn an smacht*"—*mar a dúirt an mac agus é ag bualadh a athar*). There are three elements—the quotation itself, the speaker, and the situation in which it was said. The quotation itself is always serious but becomes humorous when attributed to a certain speaker in a certain situation: "'Strength is a great thing'—as the wren said when he pulled the worm out of the frost" ("*Is iontach an rud é an neart*"—*mar a dúirt an dreoilín nuair a tharraing sé an phéist as an sioc*). My own favorite quotation proverb, given the fact that crabs walk sideways, is "'Walk straight, my son'—as the old crab said to the young crab" ("*Siúil díreach, a mhic*"—*mar a dúirt an seanphortán leis an bportán óg*). These proverbs are also known as "Wellerisms" after the character Sam Weller in Charles Dickens's *The Pickwick Papers*."

"Siúil díreach, a mhic"—mar a dúirt an seanphortán leis an bportán óg.

"Walk straight, my son"—as the old crab said to the young crab.

"Go n-éirí go geal leat"—mar a dúirt an sweep lena mhac.

"May you have a bright future"—as the chimney sweep said to his son.

"Fan go bpósfaidh tú"—mar a dúirt an fear leis an ngiorria.

"Wait until you get married"—as the man said to the hare.

"Chonaic mé cheana thú"—mar a dúirt an cat leis an mbainne te.

"I saw you before"—as the cat said to the hot milk.

"Glór mór ar bheagán olla"—mar a dúirt an t-áibhirseoir agus é ag bearradh na muice.

"A big voice with very little wool"—as the adversary (the Devil) said when he was shearing the pig.

Tramping in Co. Wicklow.

"Gluais, a mhála, is go n-éirí an t-ádh leat"—
mar a dúirt an bacach ar maidin.

"Get going, bag, and I wish you luck"—as the tramp said in the morning.

Fireside scene, Carraroe, Co. Galway.

Triads

Three things to be distrusted:
a cow's horn,
a dog's tooth
and a horse's hoof.

Three disagreeable things at home:
a scolding wife,
a squalling child
and a smoky chimney.

The three finest sights in the world:
a field of ripe wheat,
a ship in full sail
and the wife of a MacDonnell with child.

The above are examples of a form of proverb known as the triad that was very common in Irish speech and literature. There were other numerical proverbs as well but, with the exception of a small number of tetrads (groups of four), the triads alone have survived to the present day. These proverbs were, no doubt, a great aid to memory, and the popularity of the triad may well have been due to its being easily composed and memorized.

Triads occur sporadically in the literature of most other nations but do not seem to have attained the same popularity elsewhere. It has been suggested that they were so popular in Ireland and Wales that the composing of triads seemed at times to have become a sport.

A good number of triads, in Irish and in English, are still retained by the older generation in rural Ireland but it would seem that their use has greatly diminished. This section contains ten of the most popular triads from Connemara. Here is one example of a tetrad that is popular in the Ulster dialect:

San áit a mbíonn toit bíonn tine   Where there is smoke there is fire
San áit a mbíonn tine bíonn teas   Where there is fire there is heat
San áit a mbíonn teas bíonn mná   Where there is heat there are women
Agus san áit a mbíonn mná bíonn geab.   And where there are women there is gab.

Na trí nithe is géire ar bith:
Súil circe i ndiaidh gráinne
Súil gabha i ndiaidh tairne agus
Súil caillí i ndiaidh bean a mic.

The three sharpest things on earth:
A hen's eye after a grain
A blacksmith's eye after a nail and
An old woman's eye after her son's
wife.

Dublin smithy.

An old woman.

Trí nithe nach gcoinníonn a slacht i bhfad:
Teach ar ard
Capall bán
Bean bhreá.

Three things whose beauty does not
last:
A house on a hill
A white horse
A fine woman.

A white Connemara pony.

Old house, Costelloe, Co. Galway.

221

Trí chineál bia:
Bia rí ruacain
Bia tuata bairnigh
Bia caillí faochain
(Is í dá bpiocadh lena snáthaid).

Three types of food:
Cockles are a king's food
Limpets are a peasant's food
Periwinkles are an old woman's food
(And she picking them with her needle).

Periwinkles

Cockles.

Limpets.

222

Na trí rud is tapa san fharraige:
Roc, ronnach, agus rón.

The three fastest things in the sea:
Skate, mackerel, and seal.

A seal.

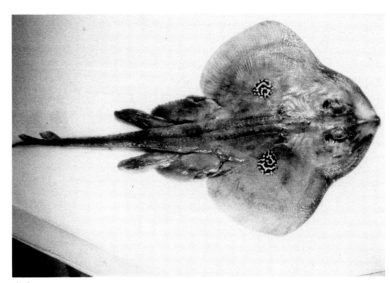

A skate.

A mackerel.

Trí ghalar gan náire:
Grá, tochas, agus tart.

Three diseases without shame:
Love, itch, and thirst.

Trí shólás an tseanduine:
Tine, tae, agus tobac.

Three comforts of an old person:
Fire, tea, and tobacco.

Interior of the house of M. Breathnach, Maam Cross, Co. Galway, in 1935.

Trí bhua an tsionnaigh:
Súil bhiorach
Cluas aireach
Eireaball scothach.

Three gifts of the fox:
A sharp eye
A careful ear
A bushy tail.

Na trí nithe is géire ar bith:
Dealg láibe
Róipín cnáibe
Focal amadáin

The three sharpest things on earth:
A thorn in the mud
A hempen rope
A fool's word.

**Triúr nach féidir leo oibriú gan cruit:
Táilliúirí, scríbhneoirí, agus cait.**

*Three who cannot work without a
hump:
Tailors, writers, and cats.*

(Humpbacked men often took up tailoring
and tailors, for this reason, were sometimes
cruelly ridiculed.)

A tailor at work, Westport, Co. Mayo.

228

Trí bhua an chait:
Léargas sa dorchadas
Siúl gan torann
Dearmad bhean an tí.

The three gifts of the cat:
Sight in the dark
Walking without noise
The housewife's mistake.

(According to legend the cat found a three-penny bit and bought the gifts for a penny each.)

Sources

An Seabhac. *Seanfhocail na Mumhan*. Baile Átha Cliath, Éire: An Gúm, 1984.

Barry, Paddy. *Voyage*. Dublin: Gill and Macmillan, 1986.

Brody, Hugh. *Inishkillane*. London: Pelican Books, 1974.

Cullen, L. M. *Life in Ireland*. New York: G. P. Putnam's Sons and London: B. T. Batsford, 1968.

Danaher, Kevin. *That's How it Was*. Dublin/Cork: Mercier Press, 1984.

Danaher, Kevin. *In Ireland Long Ago*. Dublin/Cork: Mercier Press, 1962.

Flower, Robin. *The Western Island*. London: Oxford University Press, 1944.

Greene, David. *The Irish Language*, An Ghaeilge. Dublin/Cork: Mercier Press, 1966.

Hoagland, Kathleen. *1000 Years of Irish Poetry*. New York: Grosset and Dunlap, 1962.

Jordon, John, ed. *The Pleasures of Gaelic Literature*. Dublin/Cork: Mercier Press, 1974.

Kavanagh, Patrick. *Collected Poems*. London: Martin Brian O'Keefe, 1964.

Killanin and Duignan. *The Shell Guide to Ireland*. London: Ebury Press, 1967.

Lynch, Stanislaus. "Irish Horses." *Encyclopaedia of Ireland*. Dublin: Allen Figgis, 1968.

Mac Gill, Patrick. *Children of the Dead End*. London: Caliban Books, 1985.

Mac Giollarnáth, Seán. *Annála Beaga Ó Iorrus Aithneach*. Baile Átha Cliath, Eire: Oifig an tSoláthair, 1941.

MacDonald, T. D. *Gaelic Proverbs and Proverbial Sayings*. Stirling, Scotland: Eneas Mackay, 1926.

Meyer, Kuno. *The Triads of Ireland*. Dublin: Hodges and Figgis, 1906. Vol. XIII.

Micks, W. L. *The History of the Congested Districts Board*. Dublin: Eason, 1925.

Mieder and Dundes. *The Wisdom of Many, Essays on the Proverb*. New York/London: Garland Publishing Inc., 1980.

Murphy, Séamus. *Stone Mad*. London: Routledge and Kegan Paul, 1966.

Ó Cadhain, Máirtín. *Páipéir Bhána agus Páipéir Bhreaca*. Baile Átha Cliath, Éire: An Clóchomhar, 1969.

Ó Cadhain, Máirtín. *The Road to Brightcity*. Trans. Eoghan Ó Tuairisc. Dublin: Poolbeg Press, 1981.

Ó Catháin, Séamus. *The Bedside Book of Irish Folklore*. Dublin/Cork: Mercier Press, 1980.

Ó Conaill, Seán. *Seán Ó Conaill's Book*. Baile Átha Cliath, Éire: Bhéaloideas Éireann, 1981.

Ó Conghaile, Mícheál. *Conamara agus Árainn 1880–1980, Gnéithe den Stair Shóisialta*. Conamara, Co. na Gaillimhe, Éire: Cló Iar-Chonnachta, 1988.

Ó Conghaile, Mícheál. *Gaeltacht Ráth Cairn*. Conamara, Co. na Gaillimhe, Éire: Cló Iar-Chonnachta, 1986.

Ó Conghaile, Seán. *Cois Fharraige le mo Linnse*. Baile Átha Cliath, Éire: Clódhanna Tta., 1974.

Ó hEithir, Breandán. *This is Ireland*. Dublin: The O'Brien Press, 1987.

Ó Máille, Tomás S. *Seanfhocla Chonnacht*. Baile Átha Cliath, Éire: Oifig an tSoláthair, 1948/52. Vols. I, II.

Ó Maoláin, Peadar. *Paddy Val Dhubh*. Co. na Gaillimhe, Éire: P. Ó Maoláin, Leitir Mealláin, 1986.

Ó Muirgheasa, Enrí. *Seanfhocail Uladh*. Baile Átha Cliath, Éire: Oifig an tSoláthair, 1976.

Ó Murchú, Máirtín. *The Irish Language*. Dublin: Department of Foreign Affairs and Bord na Gaeilge, 1985.

O'Neill, Timothy. *Life and Tradition in Rural Ireland*. London: J. M. Dent and Sons, 1977.

O'Rahilly, Thomas F. *A Miscellany of Irish Proverbs*. Dublin: Talbot Press, 1976.

O'Rourke, Brian. *Blas Meala/A Sip from the Honey Pot*. Dublin: Irish Academic Press, 1985.

Orwell, George. *Animal Farm*. London: Secker and Warburg, 1945.

Ó Siadhail, Mícheál. *Learning Irish*. New Haven/London: Yale University Press, 1988.

Ó Súilleabháin, S. and Christiansen, R. Th. *The Types of Irish Folktale*. Helsinki, 1963.

Ó Súilleabháin, Seán. *Irish Wake Amusements*. Dublin/Cork: Mercier Press, 1967.

Ó Súilleabháin, Seán. "People of the Roads." *Encyclopaedia of Ireland*. Dublin/Cork: Mercier Press, 1968.

O'Sullivan, Seán. *Legends from Ireland*. London: B. T. Batsford, 1977.

Ó Tuama/Kinsella. *An Duanaire*. Dublin: Dolmen Press, 1981.

Sayers, Peig. *An Old Woman's Reflections*. London: Oxford University Press, 1972.

Sayers, Peig. *Peig*. Dublin: Talbot Press, 1974.

Scott, Richard. *The Galway Hooker*. Dublin: Ward River Press, 1983.

Shaw-Smith, David. *Ireland's Traditional Crafts*. London: Thames and Hudson, 1984.

Synge, J. M. "Riders to the Sea." *Four Plays and the Aran Islands*. London: Oxford University Press, 1962.